AN ANTHOLOGY
OF REMARKABLE

Bugs

Written by Jess French

Illustrated by Angela Rizza
and Daniel Long

Introduction

Bugs run the world! Without them to break down waste, move soil, pollinate plants, control pests, carry seeds, and provide food for bigger creatures, nothing else on Earth would work. They are crucial to life as we know it — and they often go unnoticed. But bugs deserve to be celebrated. They have existed on our planet for hundreds of millions of years and have evolved to survive in almost every environment imaginable — they also possess some of the world's most extraordinary superpowers.

Many of the bugs that you will meet in these pages are big, bold, and impossible to miss, but others are more rarely seen, as they have perfected the art of concealment. Some of them fly, some crawl, some carry deadly diseases, and others may hold the keys to curing them, but every one has a fascinating story to tell. So let's take a closer look at some of our planet's most remarkable beings…

Jess French
Author

Contents

Fried egg earthworm 4

Johnston's whip spider 6

Queen Alexandra's birdwing 8

Altas moth 10

Leopard slug 12

Giant West African snail 14

Mediterranean medicinal leech 16

Pink underwing moth 18

Metamorphosis 20

Hickory horned devil 22

Grant's sun spider 24

Giant vinegaroon 26

Tarantulas 28

Flagtail centipede 30

Oleander hawk moth 32

Long-tailed giant ichneumon wasp ... 34

Devil's flower mantis 36

Legs 38

Brown forest harvestman 40

Deathstalker 42

Cockroaches 44

Indonesian leaf insect 46

Camouflage 48

Peanut bug 50

Black fat-tailed scorpion 52

Green metalwing 54

Ogre-faced spider 56

Phantom flutterer 58

Orchid mantis 60

European mole cricket 62

Green skipper 64

Glasswing butterfly 66

Soil termite 68

Marsh crane fly 70

Eciton army ant 72

Lichen katydid 74

Black beauty stick insect 76

New Zealand velvet worm 78

Picasso moth 80

Trilobite beetle 82

Saddleback caterpillar 84

Australian horror moth 86

Asian dune cricket 88

Pharaoh cicada 90

Wheel bug 92

Southern flannel moth 94

European hornet 96

Long-horned orb weaver 98

Brown-lipped snail 100

Giant frog-legged beetle 102

Scarab beetles 104

Spotted-wing antlion 106

Wasp mantidfly 108

Shocking pink dragon millipede 110

Warning colours 112

Giant robber fly 114

Violet oil beetle 116

Bullet ant 118

Black and yellow mud dauber 120

Striped scorpionfly 122

Giraffe weevil 124

Isopods 126

Silverfish 128

Common glowworm 130

Giant strong-nosed stink bug 132

Torreya trapdoor spider 134

Blue carpenter bee 136

Grasshoppers 138

Golden-bloomed grey longhorn beetle ... 140

Japanese giant water bug 142

Eggs 144

Common green lacewing 146

Namib desert beetle 148

European honeybee 150

Wheel spider 152

Gold-necked carrion beetle 154

Velvet ants 156

Australian honeypot ant 158

Bolas spider 160

Common earwig 162

Pied hoverfly 164

Tsetse fly 166

Seven-spot ladybird 168

Red weaver ant-mimicking spider 170

Common horsefly 172

Two-coloured mason bee 174

Castor bean tick 176

Spotted regal sawfly 178

Redback spider 180

Malaysian stalk-eyed fly 182

Acorn weevil 184

Yellow fever mosquito 186

Pupae 188

Golden tortoise beetle 190

Meadow froghopper 192

Sea skater 194

Bristle-tailed planthopper 196

Cochineal 198

Slender springtail 200

Pea aphid 202

House pseudoscorpion 204

Banana lacewing bug 206

Cat flea 208

Varroa mite 210

Tree of life 212

Glossary 214

Visual guide 216

Acknowledgements 224

Fried egg earthworm

Earthworms have a simple but extremely important job. They gobble up dead plants and poo out a rich soil that contains the nutrients plants need to grow. Many earthworms also have a simple appearance, but not the fried egg earthworm. It is a deep, inky blue and covered in splotches that look unbelievably like fried eggs.

This brightly-coloured creature doesn't act at all like other worms. Instead of burrowing underground, it wriggles about on the surface, squirming its way through the leaf litter. Scientists still don't know much about it — it was first discovered in 2001 in the Philippines — but we do know that it can grow extremely large and at some stages of its life it may even climb trees!

Fried egg earthworm, Philippines. The unusual pattern of the fried egg earthworm may be a way to break up its outline to hide it from predators.

This beautiful worm can grow more than 30 cm (1 ft) in length!

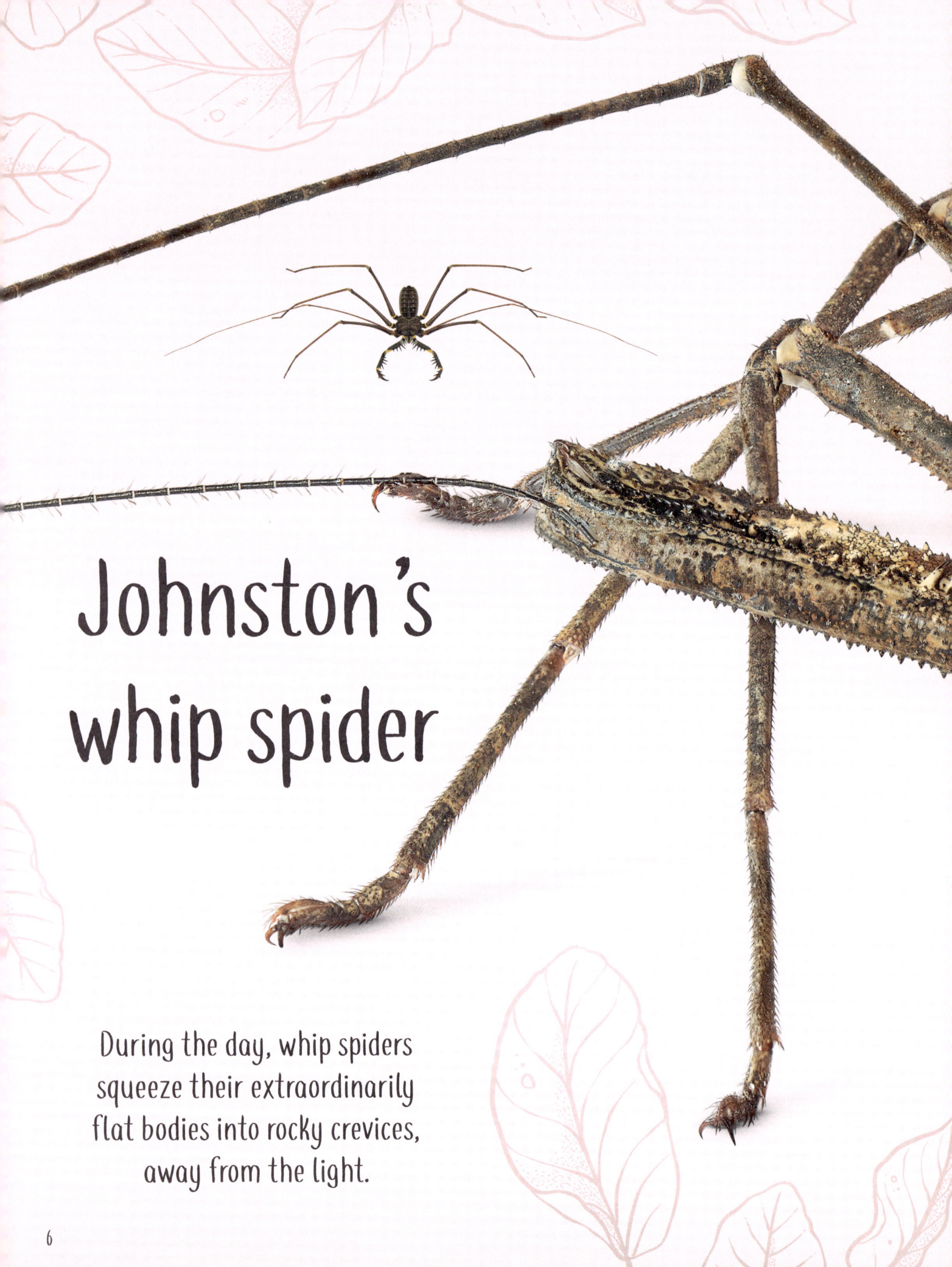

Johnston's whip spider

During the day, whip spiders squeeze their extraordinarily flat bodies into rocky crevices, away from the light.

With spiny pincers and scuttling legs, at first glance you might find whip spiders frightening. But do not fear — although they are related to scorpions and spiders, they aren't venomous. They belong to a group called amblypygids. These shy creatures spend their days hidden away in cool, dark spots in rainforests and caves, only coming out at night.

Whip spiders get their name from their long, whip-like front legs. These are also their superpower. Never used for walking, these legs are super sensitive and are instead used to feel and smell in the dark as a whip spider hunts for small insects. When it does detect prey, the whip spider uses its pincers to quickly grab the creature and gobble it up.

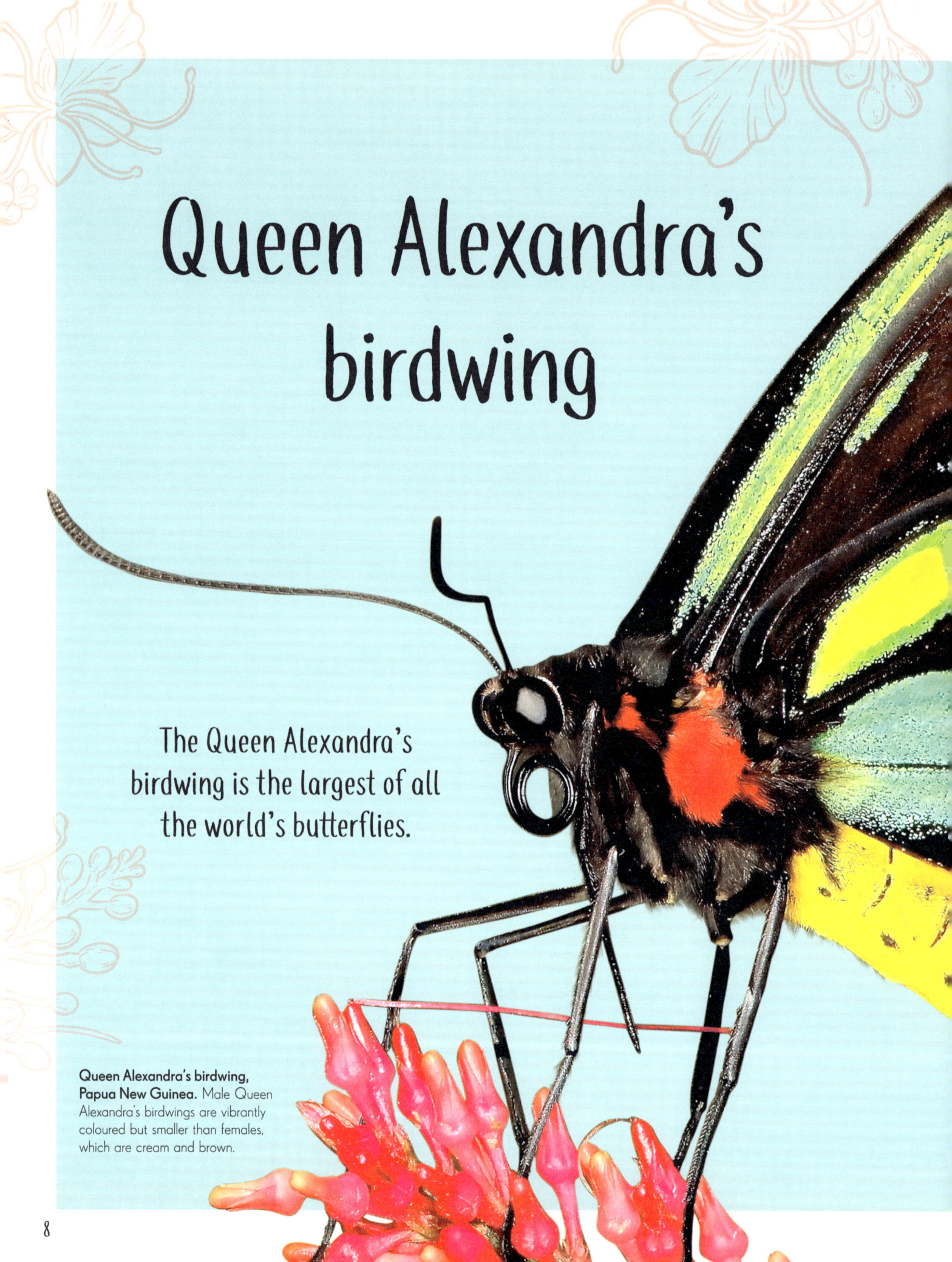

Queen Alexandra's birdwing

The Queen Alexandra's birdwing is the largest of all the world's butterflies.

Queen Alexandra's birdwing, Papua New Guinea. Male Queen Alexandra's birdwings are vibrantly coloured but smaller than females, which are cream and brown.

Male

Female

Imagine a butterfly with the wingspan of a blackbird and a body as long as a teaspoon. That's the Queen Alexandra's birdwing. There's only one place in the world where you can encounter them in the wild — the forests of Papua New Guinea. Enormous and beautiful, they flutter about, occasionally coming to land on a flower and unfurling their long proboscis to drink. The first British explorer to encounter these butterflies was Albert Meek. In 1906, he spotted one up in the treetops, out of reach of his net. So, he shot it to the ground! He took it back to England with him and that butterfly, with the bullet hole in its wing, is still kept at the Natural History Museum in London.

Atlas moth

With wings that stretch wider than a human hand, this moth is enormous! Perhaps that's why it was given the name "atlas", which was the name of an ancient Greek god who was tasked with holding up the sky for all of eternity. Other theories suggest that it was given this name because the patterns on its wings look a bit like a paper map.

Despite their great size, atlas moths never eat. Their tiny proboscis is too small to suck up nectar, so they must survive only on the energy reserves they stored up as a caterpillar. With such huge wings to power, atlas moths usually only live for one or two weeks — just enough time to mate and lay eggs.

Atlas moths are nocturnal, swooping through the night skies in search of a mate.

Atlas moth, Asia. Male atlas moths have wide, feathery antennae, which help them to find females.

Leopard slug

In a damp, shady woodland, a long, squashy creature slithers from log to log on a shimmering trail of slime. Its snazzy patterning and striking colours make it unmistakable — it's a leopard slug! Like all slugs, it needs a damp environment to survive. Unlike a snail, it cannot hide in a shell, so it must cover itself in a layer of sticky mucus to cushion itself from sharp objects and to stop itself from drying out.

Occasionally, two leopard slugs can be found tangled together, hanging from a rope of slime! This impressive feat is part of their courtship ritual. Slugs are both male and female at the same time, and after their dance is over, each will lay a large cluster of eggs.

Leopard slug, Europe.
Four tentacles at the front of
a slug's head help it to see,
smell, taste, and feel.

Slugs breathe through a hole behind
their head, usually found on
the right side of their body.

The giant West African snail can grow
to be 20 cm (8 in) long!

**Giant West African snail,
western Africa.** A snail's body
is one long foot, which glides
along on a trail of mucus.

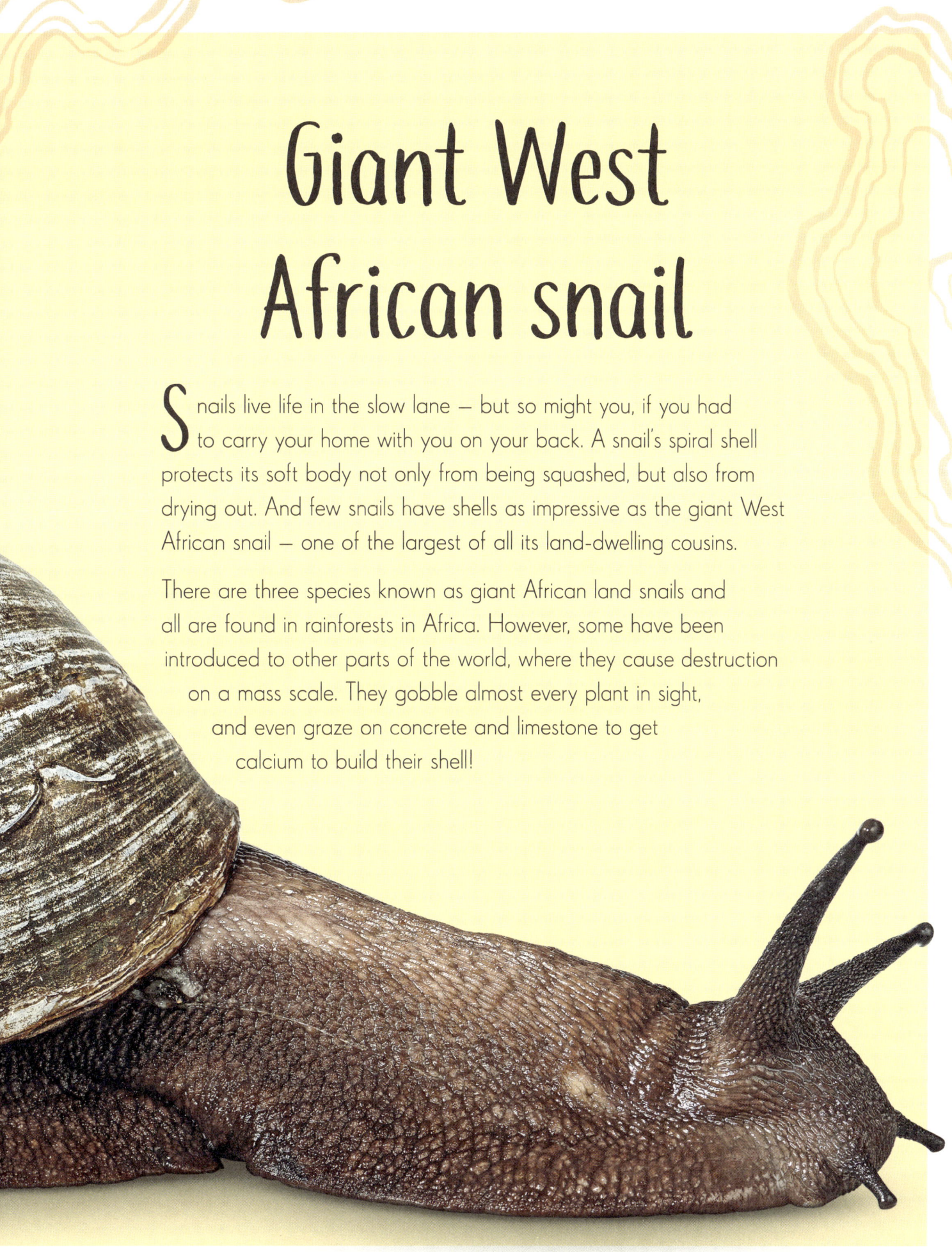

Giant West African snail

Snails live life in the slow lane — but so might you, if you had to carry your home with you on your back. A snail's spiral shell protects its soft body not only from being squashed, but also from drying out. And few snails have shells as impressive as the giant West African snail — one of the largest of all its land-dwelling cousins.

There are three species known as giant African land snails and all are found in rainforests in Africa. However, some have been introduced to other parts of the world, where they cause destruction on a mass scale. They gobble almost every plant in sight, and even graze on concrete and limestone to get calcium to build their shell!

Mediterranean medicinal leech

Mediterranean medicinal leech, western Asia and Europe. Leeches have a sucker at both ends to help them get around. They can stretch and squash their body to move.

How would you feel about having a blood-sucking worm on your arm? For thousands of years, leeches have been used by doctors to help remove blood from patients. They're perfect for the job, having already spent around 300 million years feeding on blood from other animals!

In the wild, leeches wait quietly in damp vegetation with their tail sucker gripping a leaf, while their head sucker reaches out until a potential host walks past. Each leech has not one, not two, but three sets of sharp, toothy jaws, which can pierce skin easily. However, their bites often go unnoticed. This is because special chemicals in the leech's saliva prevent any pain, and allow blood to flow without forming a scab.

After a good meal of blood, a leech can survive for over a year without feeding.

Pink underwing moth

Look at those huge eyes! Or are they eyes? The caterpillar of the pink underwing moth would make a tasty snack for rainforest birds, so it has a clever tactic to scare them away. Its neck is stamped with two huge "eyespots" and rows of what look like glistening white teeth. When it feels threatened, the caterpillar curls its head under its body, hiding its real face and revealing the huge fake eyes. These make the caterpillar look big and scary instead of small and delicious, so it can survive another day. Eventually, the caterpillar will turn into a beautiful brown moth, but it has another trick to protect itself — it can flash bright pink spots on its underwings to scare predators away.

This caterpillar feeds only on a rare plant called the carronia vine.

Pink underwing moth, Oceania. The pink underwing moth caterpillar develops its impressive eyespots as it grows.

No metamorphosis

When a silverfish hatches from its egg, it looks like a tiny version of the adult – with six legs, long antennae, and a three-pronged tail. As it grows and sheds its skin, it gets bigger and bigger, but it does not change its body shape – it does not undergo metamorphosis at all.

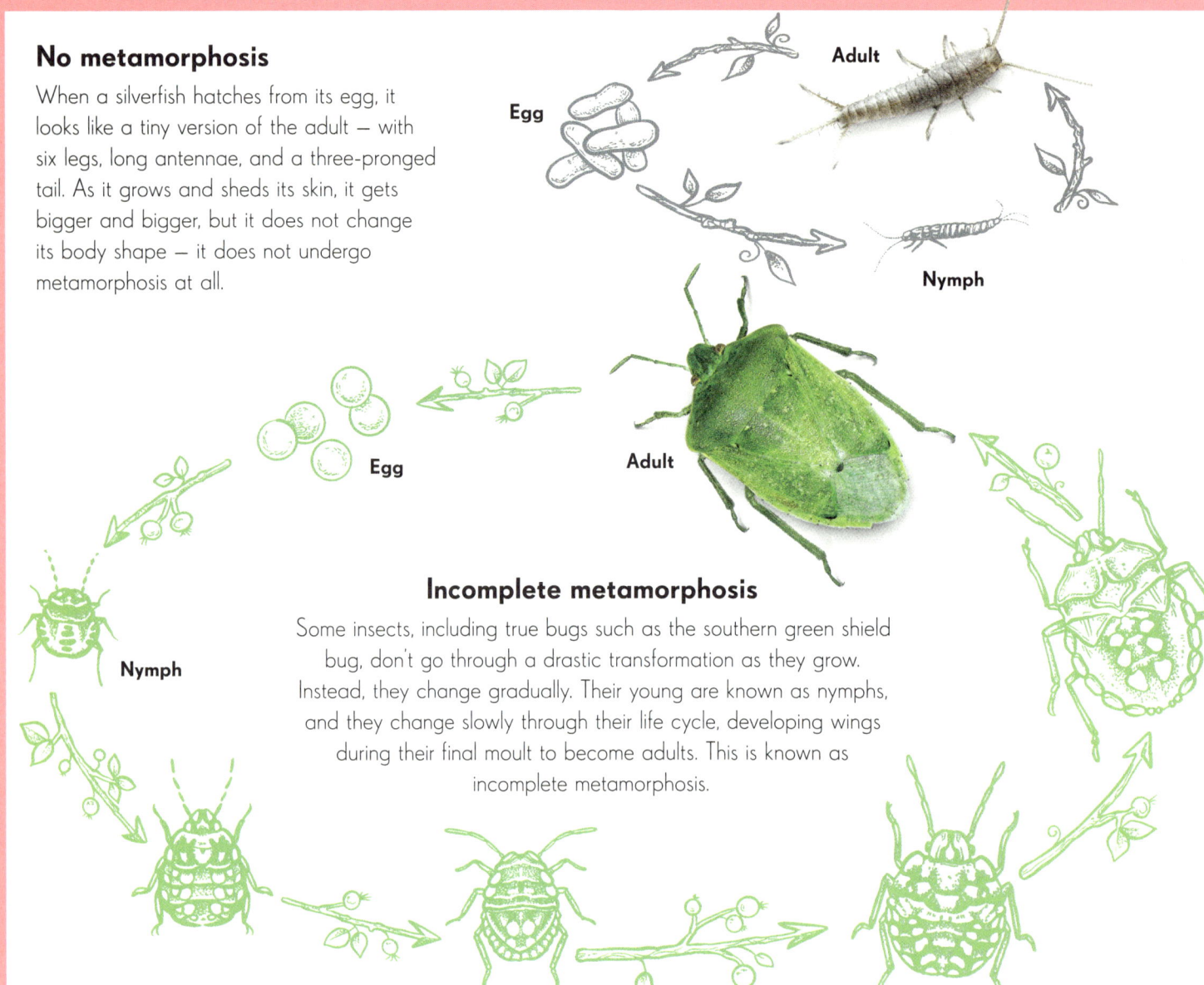

Egg

Adult

Nymph

Egg

Adult

Nymph

Incomplete metamorphosis

Some insects, including true bugs such as the southern green shield bug, don't go through a drastic transformation as they grow. Instead, they change gradually. Their young are known as nymphs, and they change slowly through their life cycle, developing wings during their final moult to become adults. This is known as incomplete metamorphosis.

Metamorphosis

Bugs sometimes start their life looking one way, then change their body shape to become something totally different. For some insects, the change can be dramatic. For others, it's more subtle. In these cases, the adult still looks largely the same as it did when it was young, but usually grows a few extra features, such as wings. When insects change body shape like this, it is called metamorphosis. Sometimes, young bugs live in a totally different environment to the adults they will become – some flying insects even start their lives underwater!

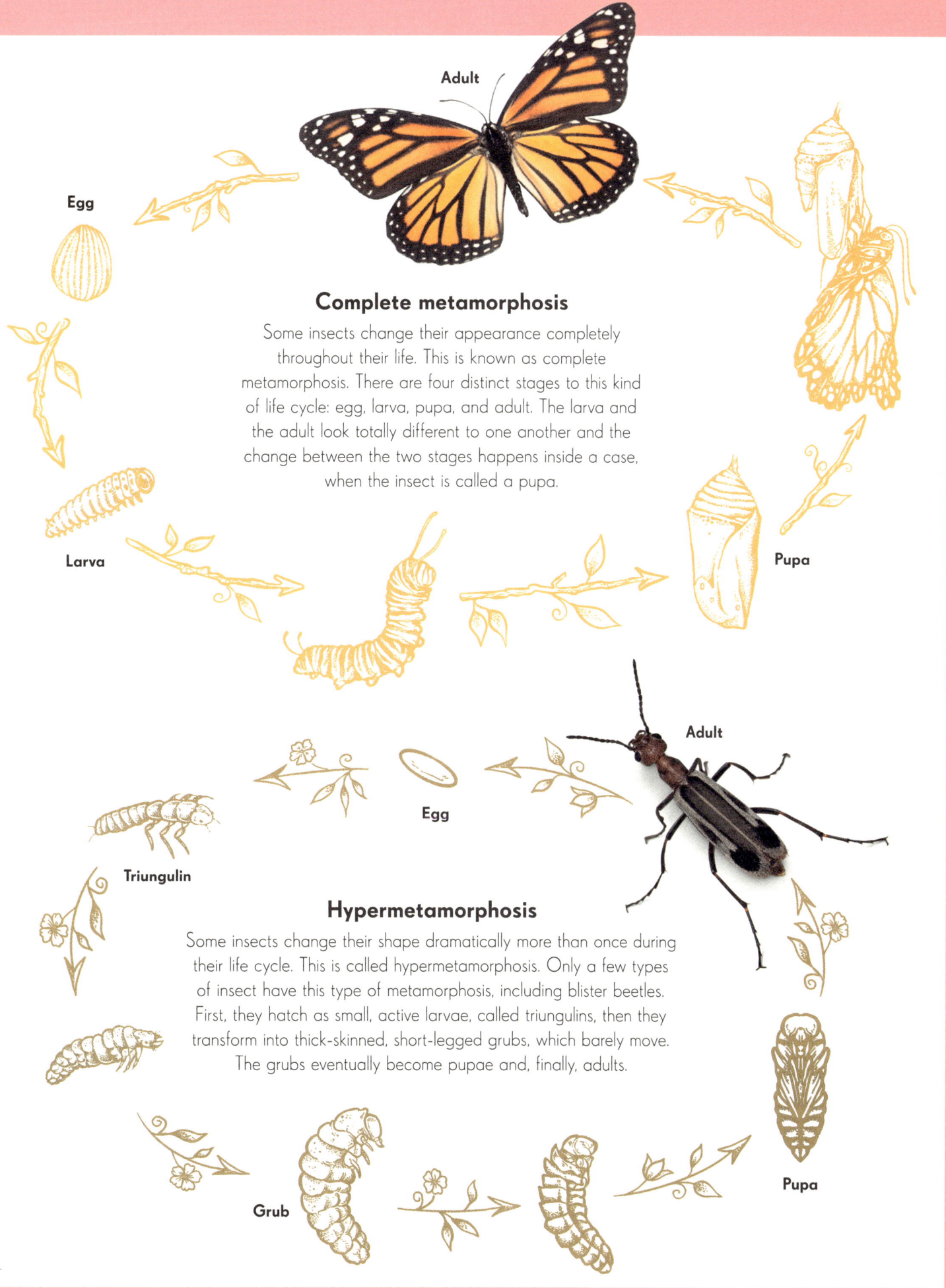

Adult

Egg

Larva

Complete metamorphosis

Some insects change their appearance completely throughout their life. This is known as complete metamorphosis. There are four distinct stages to this kind of life cycle: egg, larva, pupa, and adult. The larva and the adult look totally different to one another and the change between the two stages happens inside a case, when the insect is called a pupa.

Pupa

Triungulin

Egg

Adult

Hypermetamorphosis

Some insects change their shape dramatically more than once during their life cycle. This is called hypermetamorphosis. Only a few types of insect have this type of metamorphosis, including blister beetles. First, they hatch as small, active larvae, called triungulins, then they transform into thick-skinned, short-legged grubs, which barely move. The grubs eventually become pupae and, finally, adults.

Pupa

Grub

Hickory horned devil

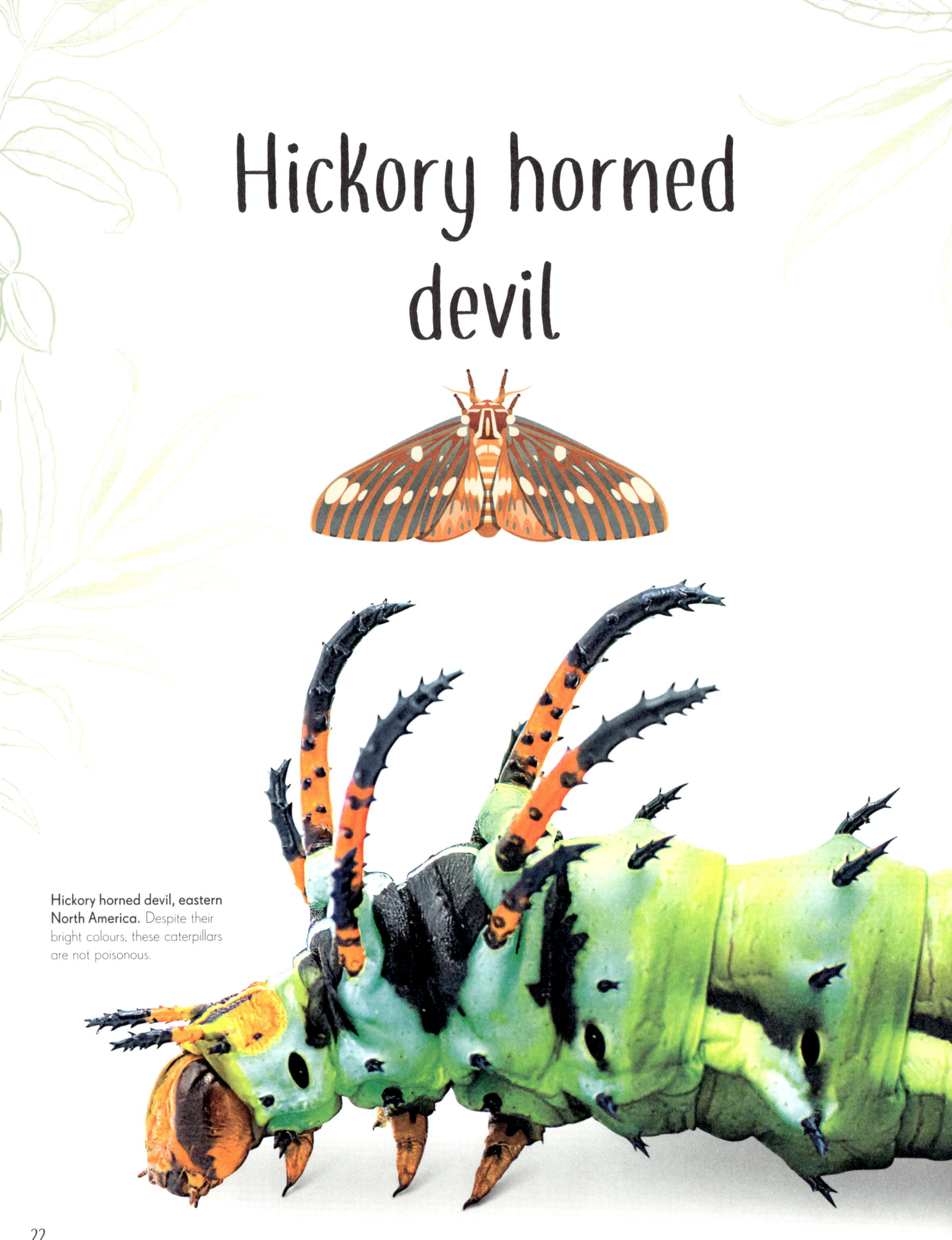

Hickory horned devil, eastern North America. Despite their bright colours, these caterpillars are not poisonous.

Usually, when we talk about caterpillars, we use the name of the butterfly or moth they will become to describe them. But the hickory horned devil is eye-catching enough to have a name of its own! As big as a hot dog, it has spectacular horns and a vibrant, green body lined with spikes.

Hickory horned devils spend most of their time munching on the leaves of hickory and walnut trees. When it is time for them to transform into adults, they inch down all the way to the ground in search of a soft patch of earth and burrow down into it. The caterpillar then becomes a pupa for around six months, before emerging as a royal walnut moth.

The hickory horned devil is both colourful as a caterpillar and as a moth.

Grant's sun spider

Look at those jaws! A sun spider's intimidating mouthparts look a bit like the claws of a crab, don't they? They are big, sharp, and perfect for tearing into large prey. Sun spiders are speedy creatures, rushing through the desert in search of food. They eat whatever they can catch: termites, beetles, wasps, scorpions, spiders, rodents, birds, lizards, and even other sun spiders.

These ferocious predators aren't actually part of the spider family, but belong to their own group called solifugids. They live in hot, dry places where they take shelter and hide during the day. But after the sun sets, they emerge, hungry, and ready to hunt for their dinner.

Sun spiders have many interesting names, including "camel spider" and "wind scorpion".

Giant vinegaroon

Do I smell salt and vinegar crisps? Oh no, it's just a disgruntled vinegaroon. Though these eight-legged relatives of scorpions might look scary, they aren't nearly as dangerous. When threatened, they spray out a fine mist of acetic acid — also known as vinegar. That might not seem like much of a defence, but their acid is 16 times more concentrated than kitchen vinegar. A squirt of it, direct to the eyes, is enough to distract a predator for long enough that the vinegaroon can scuttle away to safety. It must be a pretty effective survival technique, because vinegaroons have been found in fossils dating back to before the time of the dinosaurs!

Giant vinegaroon, southern North America. The front pair of a vinegaroon's eight legs are long and thin, and used for sensing chemicals and vibrations in its surroundings.

The vinegaroon's long tail is used
to direct its spray of acid.

Antilles pinktoe tarantula, Caribbean. The Antilles pinktoe tarantula builds funnel-shaped webs in the branches of trees and under bark.

Mexican redknee tarantula, Mexico. Mexican redknee tarantulas love to make burrows at the base of prickly cacti.

Tarantulas

When tarantulas shed their skin, everything is replaced, including their hairs and fangs.

Ornamental baboon tarantula, western Africa. This tarantula lives high up in the trees. Its beautiful pattern helps to camouflage it.

Tarantulas are large spiders that can live for up to 30 years. Their hairy bodies help them to sense the world around them, find prey, and avoid predators. When threatened, some tarantulas use their back legs to flick irritating hairs off their abdomen into the eyes of attackers.

Many tarantulas live in burrows lined with silk. They spend a lot of time in these burrows, waiting for their next meal to pass by. Tarantulas aren't fussy, they will eat anything small enough to catch. In the case of some of the larger tarantulas, this includes mammals, reptiles, and birds!

Colombian giant tarantula, northern South America. The Colombian giant tarantula lives in the rainforest and loves to burrow into the undergrowth.

Burgundy goliath bird eater, northern South America. This is one of the largest spiders on the planet!

Peacock tarantula, eastern India. The peacock tarantula cannot flick its beautiful blue hairs, but can move very fast!

Flagtail centipede, eastern Africa. Centipedes usually have one pair of legs per body segment. Flagtail centipedes can have more than 40 legs in total.

Flagtail centipede

The "flags" on the tail of a flagtail centipede are actually flattened legs!

Centipedes are not to be messed with. They are fast, aggressive and have a venomous bite. They inject their venom through curved claws at the front of their bodies. These look a lot like fangs, but they are actually special legs with venom glands attached. In its home in eastern Africa, the flagtail centipede zooms around at night, hunting down any other animals small enough for it to catch. When frightened, it will shake its unusual pink, feather-like tail and make a loud hissing sound.

Though they sound scary, centipedes also have a softer side. They are doting mothers that protect, guard, and clean their eggs and young until the nymphs are big enough to fend for themselves.

Oleander hawk moth caterpillars have startling blue spots that look like glowing eyes, which may scare away predators.

Caterpillar

Adult

Oleander hawk moth

It's a warm summer evening and the scents of honeysuckle and jasmine linger in the air. Under the gentle glow of the moon, a large moth flits between the leaves, gliding swiftly from flower to flower, like a hawk tracking its prey. Its powerful wings beat rapidly, which lets it hover, motionless in the air, in front of each bloom. Then, it uncoils its long drinking tube, called a proboscis, and sips on the flower's sweet nectar. This is the oleander hawk moth, and it will feed on nectar from any tubular flower. However, its caterpillars prefer to eat the leaves of oleander plants, which is where this species gets its name.

Oleander hawk moth, Africa, Asia, and southern Europe. The bold green and cream patterns on adult oleander hawk moths keep them camouflaged on leaves.

Long-tailed giant ichneumon wasp

Long-tailed giant ichneumon wasp, eastern North America.
A thin membrane helps push the female's long ovipositor into tough bark.

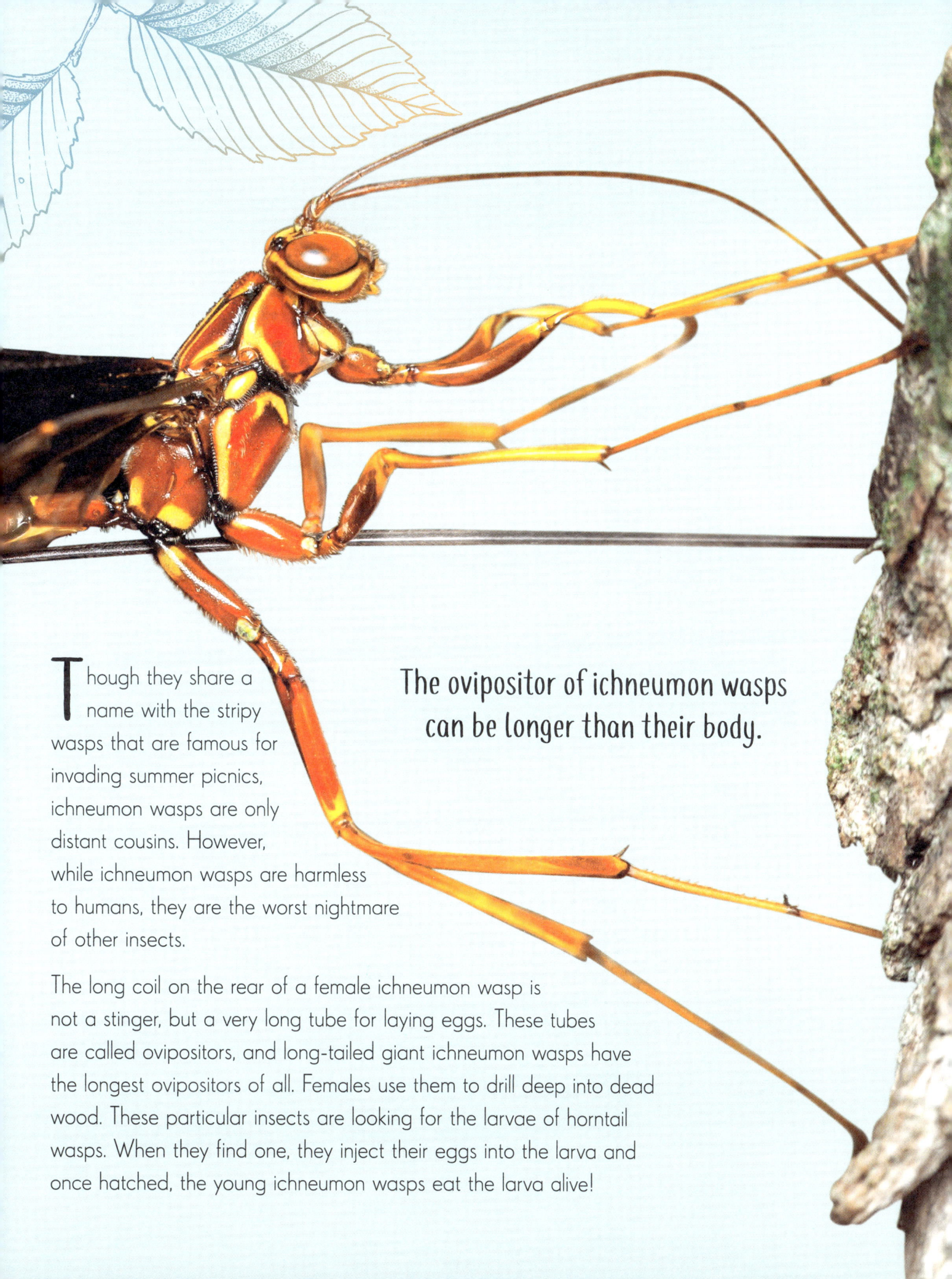

Though they share a name with the stripy wasps that are famous for invading summer picnics, ichneumon wasps are only distant cousins. However, while ichneumon wasps are harmless to humans, they are the worst nightmare of other insects.

The long coil on the rear of a female ichneumon wasp is not a stinger, but a very long tube for laying eggs. These tubes are called ovipositors, and long-tailed giant ichneumon wasps have the longest ovipositors of all. Females use them to drill deep into dead wood. These particular insects are looking for the larvae of horntail wasps. When they find one, they inject their eggs into the larva and once hatched, the young ichneumon wasps eat the larva alive!

The ovipositor of ichneumon wasps can be longer than their body.

Devil's flower mantis

Look at me! I'm so big and scary! That's what the devil's flower mantis is trying to say by waving its brightly-coloured, toothed arms over its head. Most of the time, the devil's flower mantis wants to stay hidden. It is an ambush predator that catches prey by surprise. Its clever pattern usually makes it difficult to see on plants. However, if it is attacked by another predator, the devil's flower mantis will stand up to its full height, raise its arms to reveal red flashes, and try to make itself look frightening. Those sharp spikes aren't just for show, though — they are just as effective at grabbing flying insects as they pass as scratching a predator.

Unlike other insects, mantises can spin their head all the way back both left and right, so they are always watching!

Devil's flower mantis, eastern Africa. Male devil's flower mantises have large, red antennae to help them find females.

Harlequin beetle

Both male and female harlequin beetles have very long front legs, but the males' legs are longest. They use them to fight with other males for mates, and to make themselves look big and scary to predators.

Green water boatman

Water boatmen are found in freshwater ponds and slow-moving rivers, often near the surface. Their strong, oar-shaped back legs are brilliant at powering them through the water.

Legs

When people think of bugs, legs are often the first thing that come to mind. It's not surprising, considering that many bugs have lots of them – and they are sometimes the easiest thing to see, as the creature scuttles out of sight. Many bugs are classified by the number of legs they have. Insects have six, arachnids have eight, and millipedes can have more than 1,000. In the bug world, legs are not just for walking. Hard exoskeletons allow the legs of arthropods to be used for all sorts of jobs, from leaping and digging, to swimming and fighting.

Honeybee workers pack pollen into their pollen baskets to store it safely when flying.

European honeybee

When insects visit flowers to gather nectar, they often become covered in pollen. Bees collect this pollen to feed to their young, and they have special "baskets" on their back legs to store it in!

Old world swallowtail

Caterpillars are insects, so they only have six true legs, but they also have many fleshy blobs, called prolegs, which help them to grip, grasp, and crawl. Their six true legs are found at their head end.

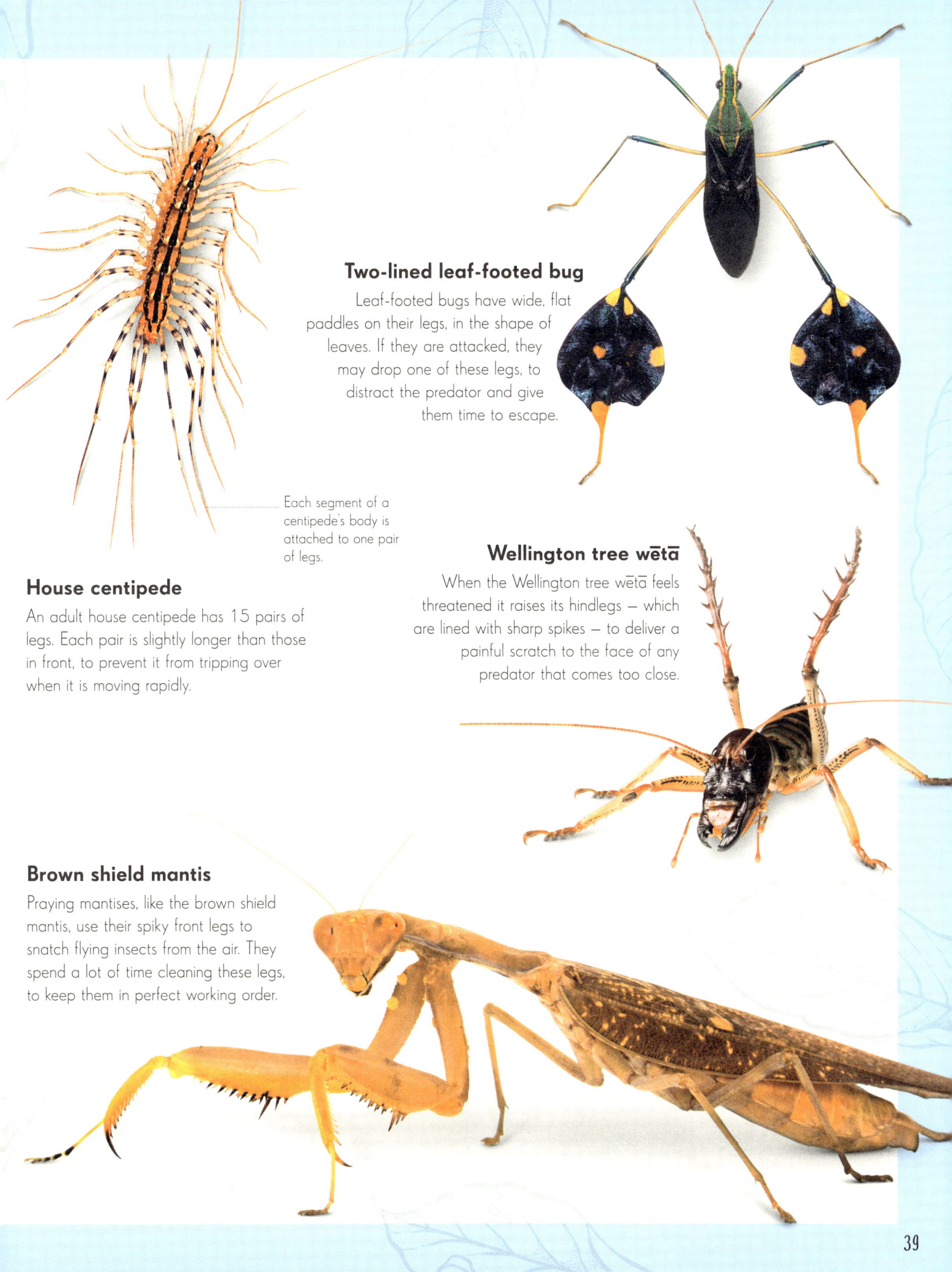

Two-lined leaf-footed bug

Leaf-footed bugs have wide, flat paddles on their legs, in the shape of leaves. If they are attacked, they may drop one of these legs, to distract the predator and give them time to escape.

Each segment of a centipede's body is attached to one pair of legs.

House centipede

An adult house centipede has 15 pairs of legs. Each pair is slightly longer than those in front, to prevent it from tripping over when it is moving rapidly.

Wellington tree wētā

When the Wellington tree wētā feels threatened it raises its hindlegs — which are lined with sharp spikes — to deliver a painful scratch to the face of any predator that comes too close.

Brown shield mantis

Praying mantises, like the brown shield mantis, use their spiky front legs to snatch flying insects from the air. They spend a lot of time cleaning these legs, to keep them in perfect working order.

Brown forest harvestman

Eight long legs make this spindly arachnid look a lot like a spider, but it's actually a harvestman. Harvestmen don't make silk, and unlike spiders, which have bodies made of two parts, they have a body made of one round ball.

Harvestmen hide in the day and come out at dusk. They only have two eyes and their eyesight is poor, though, so how do they find their way? They rely on special sensors on their second pair of legs. These legs are covered in small hairs that can taste, smell, and feel for vibrations. With these senses, harvestmen can easily wander about in the dark on their hunt for food.

If a harvestman feels threatened, it can drop a leg to distract a predator long enough for it to run away.

Brown forest harvestman, Costa Rica.
Harvestmen hang upside down to shed their skin. This harvestman has almost pulled its long legs free of its old exoskeleton.

Deathstalker, northern Africa and southwestern Asia. In its defensive pose, the deathstalker holds its pincers wide and its stinger ready to strike.

Deathstalker

Deathstalkers, like all
scorpions, glow slightly
in the light of the moon.

As the sun sets in the desert, an ancient predator scuttles out from beneath a rock. The deathstalker scorpion is a deadly hunter, even in the dark. Using its super-sensitive legs, it can feel the vibrations of small creatures scurrying nearby. When an insect ventures close enough, the deathstalker moves rapidly, grabbing the creature with its pincers and arching its stinger up over its back to deliver its deadly venom

Amazingly, the venom produced by the deathstalker could actually also be used to help people. Scientists have found that it contains a substance that could be used in medical treatments for diseases.

Hissing cockroach, Madagascar. When frightened, hissing cockroaches force air out of holes in the sides of their body called spiracles. This makes a loud hissing sound.

Domino cockroach, southern India. The black-and-white pattern of the domino cockroach is thought to make them look like an aggressive ground beetle, to scare off predators!

There are about 4,500 species of cockroach, and only 25 of those live around human homes.

Cloud forest cockroach, Central America. Many cockroaches, like this cloud forest cockroach, have large wings and can fly to escape from danger.

Emerald cockroach, eastern Asia. The magnificent emerald cockroach is beautiful but also strong, and is great at climbing.

Cockroaches

Plenty of people dislike cockroaches, but why? They don't bite or suck blood. But just the sight of them is enough to make some people squeal and run for cover. In reality, cockroaches are one of the most helpful insects on the planet! A few types live near human homes, acting like miniature caretakers by gobbling up our rubbish at night. Thousands more live in the wild. There, they dart about, munching on waste and dead plant material, breaking it down into nutrients in the soil, which allows new plants to grow. Some cockroaches even carry pollen from flower to flower, helping plants to make seeds.

Headlight cockroach, northern South America. Male headlight cockroaches have raised, orange spots behind their head.

Indonesian leaf insect

Leaf insects might have the most impressive camouflage in the whole of the animal kingdom. So good, in fact, that when early explorers saw them, they thought they had happened upon magical trees, whose leaves could walk! The leaf insect's camouflage is so effective that these usually-vegetarian creatures may occasionally nibble each other instead of the plant they are feeding on — even they can't see through the disguise.

The camouflage doesn't end there, though. Female leaf insects lay tiny, round eggs that look like seeds. When the baby leaf insect nymphs hatch, they don't look like leaves, but become more leaf-like as they grow.

Indonesian leaf insect, Indonesia. These leaf insects are all the same species, but they are different colours to camouflage themselves against living plants or dead leaves.

Nymph

Adult

Leaf insects sway in
the breeze to help add
to their disguise.

Merveille du jour

The stunning wings of the merveille du jour moth are mottled in green and brown. This helps them blend in perfectly with lichen on the trees on which they often rest.

The bold patterns on this moth's wings help to break up its outline.

Giant walkingstick

Just like some sticks, stick insects can be very long. Giant walkingsticks have been known to grow to more than 50 cm (20 in). They are also brown, walk slowly, and pretend to sway if they feel a breeze.

Camouflage

If an animal wants to avoid being eaten by a predator, or sneak up on prey, it takes much less energy to hide than to fight or run. But a truly brilliant disguise requires more than just a splash of colour. To really disappear into its surroundings, a creature might need to take on a certain shade, texture, shape, or even behaviour. Luckily, when it comes to camouflage, bugs are experts. In fact, some bugs are so good at pretending to be plants, they can be nibbled by herbivores, which were searching for juicy leaves to eat!

Giant katydid

Giant katydids are the largest of all the katydids. Their heavy body makes jumping and flying a challenge, so they rely on their excellent camouflage to protect them from harm. Their green exoskeleton and veined wing cases make them look like leaves.

Fly moth

In the running for most unusual camouflage, this moth has wings which mimic the appearance of flies feeding on dung! Many predators avoid dung-feeding flies as they can carry disease.

Bird-dropping spider

It might not be the most glamorous of the bug disguises, but most predators have no interest in snacking on piles of bird poo — which means the bird-dropping spider doesn't need to hide to be left alone.

It seems as though there is a fly on each of the fly moth's front wings.

This butterfly's wings are the same shape as a leaf. ....

Orange oakleaf butterfly

When closed, the orange oakleaf butterfly's wings look just like dead leaves! But inside is a secret… The top side of its wings are beautifully striped in orange and blue.

Flower spider

Flower spiders can change colour to match their surroundings. This helps them to sit undetected on flowers, where they wait patiently for pollinators to visit, so they can catch them to eat.

Ant-snatching assassin bug

Sometimes, effective camouflage can involve smells, too! The ant-snatching assassin bug sticks the bodies of ants it has sucked the juices from onto its back, so that its own scent is disguised.

Peanut bug

Peanut bug, southern North America
and northern South America. The
peanut bug's lizard-shaped head is
thought to scare off predators.

The peanut bug has as many different names as it does ways to defend itself! Many of its titles, including peanut-headed lanternfly, alligator bug, and jequitiranabóia (meaning "the flying snake") refer to the strange bulge on top of its head. Though it might not look exactly the same to us, it's thought that to peanut bug predators that bulge looks a lot like the head of a lizard or snake. If a pretend lizard head isn't enough to prevent it from being attacked, the peanut bug also has huge spots that resemble eyes on its hindwings, which it can flash open. And if even that doesn't work, it can squirt out a foul-smelling spray. Enough to make any sensible predator seek out an easier lunch.

Local legends say that peanut bugs have a deadly bite, but in truth they are harmless vegetarians that feed on the sap from trees.

Black fat-tailed scorpion, northern Africa and southwestern Asia. The bulb-shaped structure above the pointed stinger is called the telson. This holds the venom gland.

Scorpions love moonless nights – the darker the better for these nocturnal hunters.

Black fat-tailed scorpion

It's said that you can tell how dangerous a scorpion is by the size of its pincers and its sting. If it has huge pincers then it likely uses those more than its sting, which means its venom probably isn't that dangerous. But, if it has a huge sting and tiny pincers… Watch out! Its sting is likely to be pretty potent.

What if a scorpion's whole tail is thick and chunky, though? In the case of the black fat-tailed scorpion, it means it's one of the most dangerous scorpions in the world! Not only is its venom highly toxic, it is also very aggressive, meaning it is more likely to sting than run away if it is disturbed.

Green metalwing

A damselfly's four wings work individually — each one can move in a different direction.

Damselflies have unbelievable flying skills. They can fly forwards, backwards, hover, and dive. They can even fly upside down! This is only possible because of their incredible wings. If you looked closely, you would see that damselfly wings are supported by a network of long, thin tubes, called veins. These veins are like the skeleton of the wing, they make it strong and stable. Between the veins is a thin material, a bit like skin, called a membrane. This layer is light and flexible, and helps the damselfly to cut speedily through the air. In many damselflies, this layer is see-through, but the male green metalwing has hindwings that shimmer green and blue in the sunlight.

Green metalwing, eastern Asia and Southeast Asia. This close-up of one of a male green metalwing's hindwings shows the network of veins and brilliant green membrane.

Ogre-faced spider

Building a web and waiting for lunch to fly into it is just one of the incredible ways that spiders use their silk. Ogre-faced spiders, also known as net-casting spiders, have a more direct approach. At night they dangle head-down from a plant, with a net of dense, sticky silk held between their four front legs. They may wait, totally still, for many hours for something tasty to wander past. When at last it does, the ogre-faced spider doesn't waste a moment! It springs into action, plunging downwards with its net outstretched, to capture the prey in its blanket of silk. This unique hunting strategy can also be used to capture flying insects mid-air.

Ogre-faced spider, Cameroon.
Ogre-faced spiders use their enormous eyes to spot their prey in the dark.

Ogre-faced spiders have the biggest eyes of any spider! Do you think they look like an ogre?

Phantom flutterer

Phantom flutterers can fly forwards, backwards, and upside down.

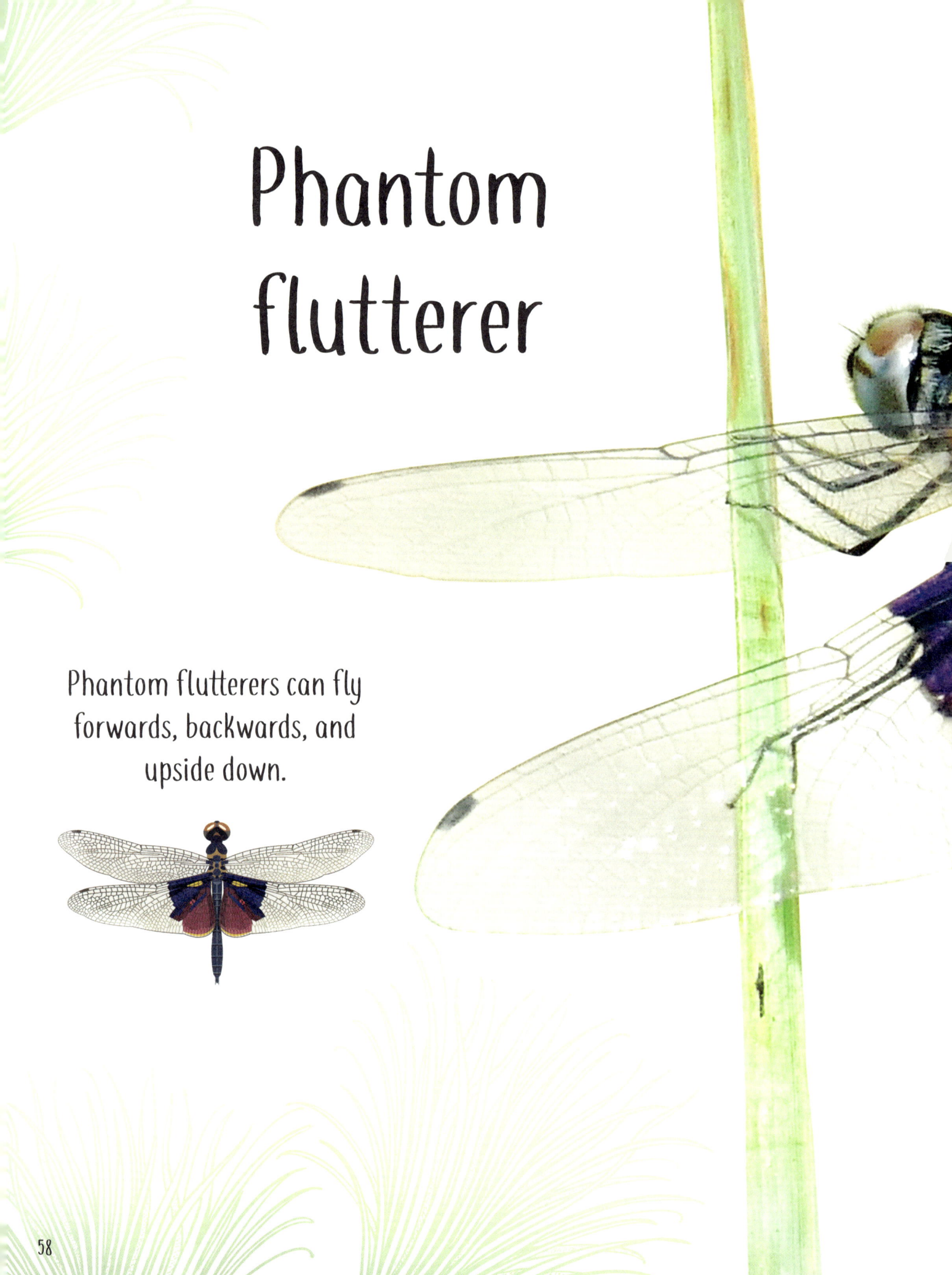

Phantom flutterer, Africa and southwestern Asia. When not in flight, phantom flutterers can often be found resting on sunny waterside perches.

Dragonflies are fearsome hunters. They zip quickly through the air with four large wings that glisten in the sunlight. If a dragonfly locks onto a target, it almost never misses. Its large eyes hone in on its prey before it grabs its dinner with spiky arms.

There are around 7,000 species of dragonfly, but phantom flutterers are one of the most distinctive. It's easy to spot the striking patch on their hindwings, which makes them look like they've been splashed with metallic paint! But what really sets them apart is the graceful way they move - fluttering their wings like ghostly butterflies.

Orchid mantis

Nymph

Adult

When early explorers first came across the orchid mantis, they thought it was the bloom of a fly-catching plant.

What a beautiful flower. But look again. The pink and white orchid mantis, with its wide, flat legs, is perfectly disguised to sit on the stem of a plant and look exactly like a flower. Its appearance is so convincing that hungry insects find it irresistible, swooping in for a slurp of tasty nectar. At this moment, the mantis strikes! It snatches the insect from the air with sharp, spiked arms, and eats it alive.

Despite its name, the orchid mantis will happily impersonate a wide range of other flowers. These beautiful assassins don't always look like blooms, though. When orchid mantis nymphs first hatch from their egg, their colours are a vibrant black-and-orange — in the animal kingdom, these colours mean "Watch out, I'm deadly!".

Orchid mantis, Southeast Asia.
Other insects struggle to tell the difference between an orchid mantis and a real flower.

European mole cricket

A mole cricket's song can be heard from a distance of four football pitches away!

Beneath our feet, there's an underground world filled with incredible creatures. Many, like the European mole cricket, are perfectly adapted for life in the soil. Look at its wide, flat hands. Do they remind you of another burrowing animal? Just like a mole, the European mole cricket uses those strong paddles to tunnel its way through the ground in search of worms, grubs, and roots to eat. Unlike a mole, though, mole crickets sing to attract a mate. Male mole crickets dig a special sound chamber at the entrance of their burrow, which makes their chirrups even louder, and start to sing. This attracts females, which — perhaps surprisngly — use their wings to fly towards the sound to find their mate.

European mole cricket, northern Africa, western Asia, and Europe. The European mole cricket uses its wide hands to dig burrows that can be 1 m (3 ft) deep.

When it emerges from its chrysalis,
a butterfly's proboscis is in two parts,
but they soon join together.

Green skipper

Flying is hungry work, every wing beat requires a huge amount of energy. That's why butterflies usually rely on very sugary food sources, such as fruit juice or nectar. The green skipper butterfly is no different. It stops regularly whilst flying to snack on nectar. But plants often hide this sweet treat deep inside their flowers, so butterflies need an extra special trick to get to it. Instead of biting mouthparts, they have a long, thin tube that curls up neatly under their head. It's called a proboscis and it's what butterflies use to feed. Like a drinking straw, it is hollow in the middle and it's thin enough to slip inside even long blooms to get to the nutritious nectar.

Green skipper, northern Caribbean. When not drinking, butterflies coil up their proboscis into a neat spiral.

Glasswing butterfly

Many animals take on the colouring of their surroundings to disguise themselves from hungry predators, but very few are see-through! Being transparent is the ultimate camouflage — it means being hard to spot in any environment, which is very handy for a butterfly that can be found in many different places. Living across the Americas, glasswing butterflies are most commonly found in the shade of mountain rainforests, but they can travel up to 19 km (12 miles) a day up and down the slopes.

Both glasswing butterflies and their caterpillars like to feed on poisonous plants. They store the toxic chemicals in their bodies as a defence. Male glasswings also use these chemicals to create a perfume that attracts females.

A special wax coats the wings of a glasswing butterfly, to stop them from being too shiny.

Glasswing butterfly, southern North America and northern South America. Glasswings look as if they only have four legs because the front pair is smaller than in other butterflies.

Soil termite

The queens of some termite species can live for more than 20 years!

Queen

Worker

Soldier

Soil termite, Southeast Asia.
A queen soil termite's body can grow as large as a child's finger. She can hold thousands of eggs in her body.

Soil termites are extraordinary builders. They live in huge mounds, which they create themselves by sticking together globs of soil, saliva, and plant matter. Inside their nest, these termites farm fungus to eat! They gather wood from their surroundings and bring it underground for the fungus to grow on.

Termites live in huge communities, and every member of the colony has an important role to play. Soldiers are large, with sharp mouthparts. If provoked, they will attack. Workers are smaller. They are responsible for gathering food and building the nest. The most important termite in the colony is the queen. She lays eggs that hatch into more soldiers and workers so the colony can grow.

Marsh crane fly

Like all flies, a crane fly's hindwings
have turned into weights on stalks
that help them balance when flying.

With their long, delicate legs and slender bodies, it's easy to see why some people give crane flies the nickname "daddy longlegs"! They are found in all kinds of different habitats — in woods and fields, and by streams and ponds — but you might spot them in your home too. Bright lights attract them into buildings, and once inside they are hard to miss as they bump into windows and doors.

Adult crane flies only live for a couple of weeks, just enough time to find a mate and lay eggs. Those eggs hatch into squirming, wormlike larvae, which live underground. The larvae are often called "leatherjackets", due to their leatherlike, brown exoskeleton.

Marsh crane fly, northern Africa and Europe. Crane flies are often mistaken for mosquitoes, but they are completely harmless.

Eciton
army ant

Soldier army ants have enormous, hook-shaped jaws that they use to protect the colony from predators.

Queen

Worker

Soldier

What's that flowing through the forest? Is it a river? No, it's millions of insects marching over the forest floor, overwhelming and gobbling everything in their path. This can only be a colony of army ants. Army ants have no permanent nest because they are almost always on the move. After a busy day of marching through the forest, they rest wherever they stop when night falls. To create a temporary nest, they use an incredible material - their own bodies! The worker ants link themselves into a structure called a bivouac (bih-voo-ak) to protect the queen and her young. This gives shelter to the most precious members of the colony. And, in the morning, they simply unlink themselves and head off for another day.

Eciton army ant, southern North America and northern South America. Eciton army ants communicate with one another through chemical signals.

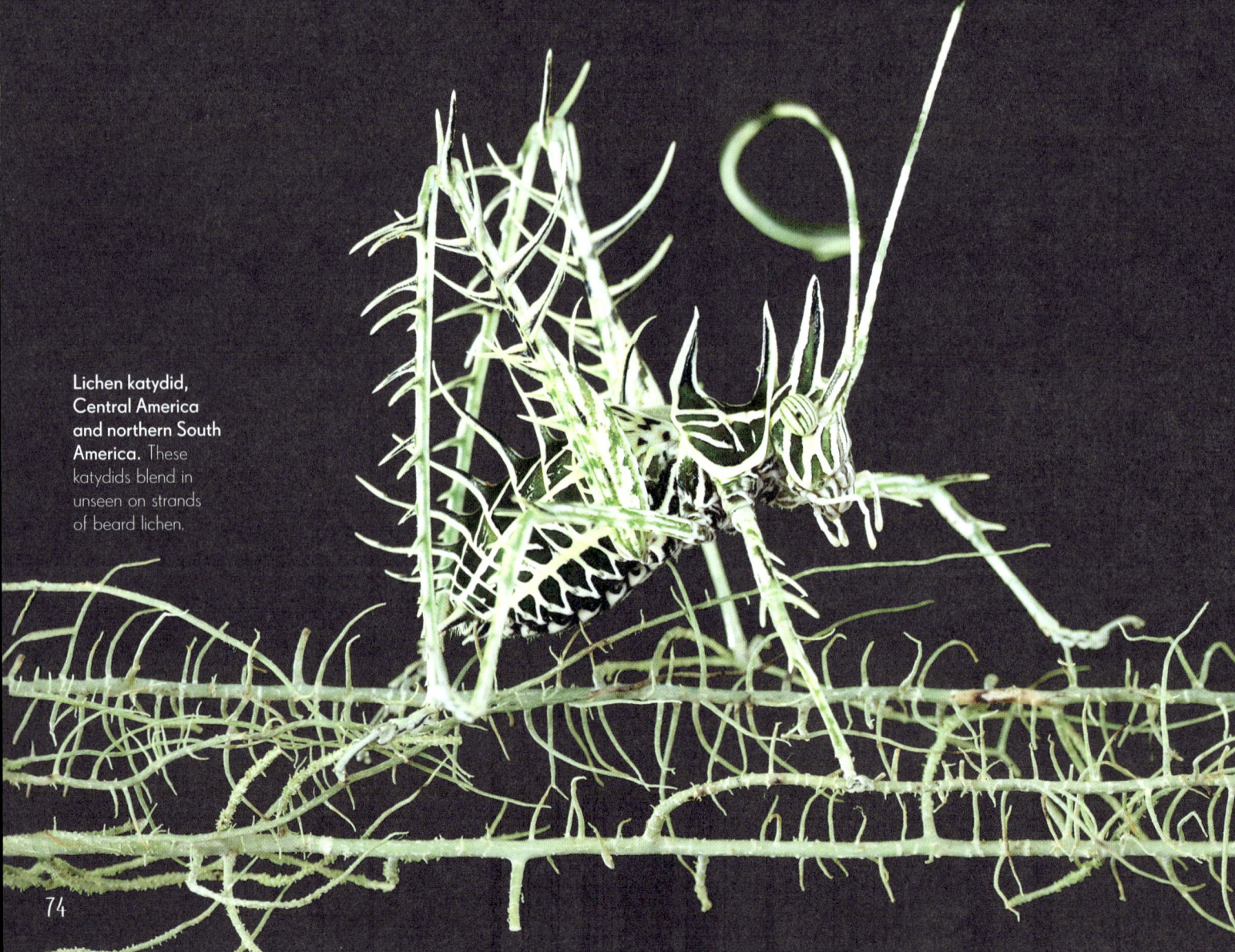

Lichen katydid, Central America and northern South America. These katydids blend in unseen on strands of beard lichen.

Like crickets and grasshoppers,
katydids sing loudly to communicate
with each other.

Black beauty stick insect

Black beauty stick insect, Peru. When frightened, black beauty stick insects raise their brightly-coloured wings.

A tiny patch of Peruvian rainforest, high in the Cordillera del Cóndor mountain range, is the only place in the wild you will find these rare and beautiful stick insects. Their forest home is rich in life and supports an astonishing number of other plants and animals — including some that have only just been found! Under the cover of darkness, black beauty stick insects march over the branches of pepper trees, gobbling up leaves. Their velvety black exoskeleton keeps them hidden in the shadows of the night. If a predator approaches though, they may flash open their vibrant red wings and release a puff of stinky gas to frighten the attacker away.

These insects are sometimes called golden-eye stick insects, due to their bright yellow eyes.

New Zealand
velvet worm

New Zealand velvet worm, New Zealand. These velvet worms usually have between 13 and 16 pairs of legs, which end in sharp claws that help them to grip and climb.

Velvet worms dry out easily,
so they hide away from the
sun in damp, dark places.

What could this creature be? An unusual squishy centipede? A small snake with legs? It's actually a velvet worm, which are quite unlike any other animal. Velvet worms have a soft body and many legs, and a deadly secret… Small nozzles on either side of their head act like slime guns, firing out streams of sticky mucus! But what use is this strange weapon? When a velvet worm feels threatened by a predator, or if it spots a bug it fancies to eat, it shoots them with a quick-drying glue, trapping them in place. This gives the velvet worm just enough time to wriggle away to safety — or to suck out its prey's juices for lunch.

Picasso moth, southern Asia and Southeast Asia. The dots and lines on this moth's wings break up its outline and make it more difficult to spot.

The Picasso moth is nocturnal and feeds on nectar.

Picasso moth

Has someone splashed this moth with paint? It might look like a colourful artwork by the artist Picasso, but the lines and blotches on the wings of this moth are completely natural. We often think of moths as dull and drab, but the Picasso moth proves that they can be bright and eye-catching, too! Both butterflies and moths get their colours from tiny scales on their wings. Each wing is covered in thousands of these scales, and the colour we see when we look at them is all to do with how they reflect light. The scales are also important for flying as they help air to flow smoothly over the wing.

Trilobite beetle

Trilobite beetles are named after a prehistoric ocean creature called a trilobite.

Female trilobite beetles look like they are from a prehistoric world — like they might have once been found scuttling between the legs of a Velociraptor. But they are actually quite modern beetles, first appearing long after the dinosaurs had died out.

These beetles are well protected, with three wide, armoured plates behind their head and a train of smaller segments, which are sometimes covered in spines. Unlike most beetles, which start their lives as larvae that look very different to the adults, female trilobite beetles keep the same body shape throughout their life. Male trilobite beetles don't have this amazing coat of armour and are smaller, but do have wings.

Saddleback caterpillar

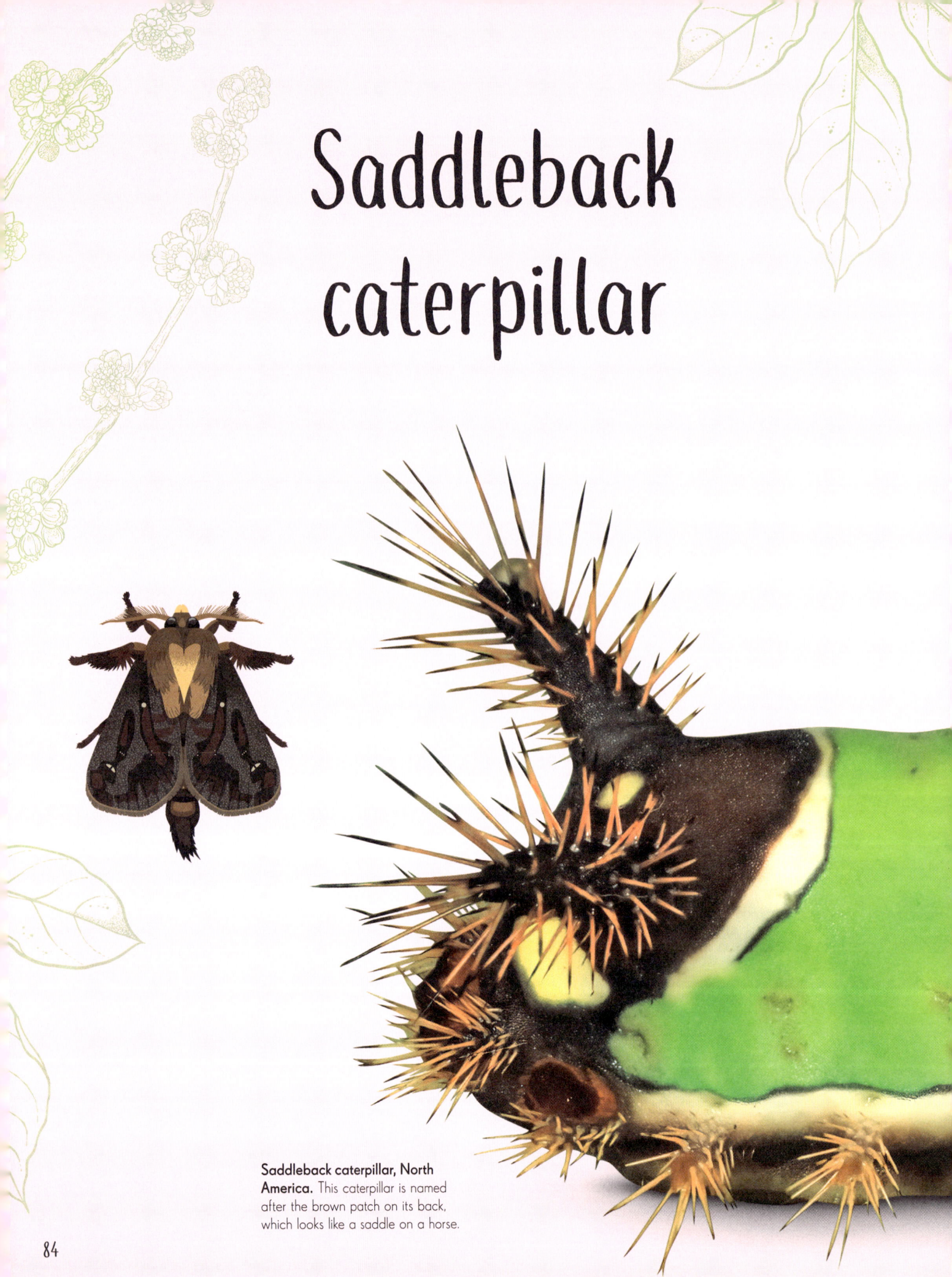

Saddleback caterpillar, North America. This caterpillar is named after the brown patch on its back, which looks like a saddle on a horse.

Do not touch this caterpillar! Though saddleback caterpillars look appealing with bright colours, their quill-like spikes are designed to break off into the skin of predators, where they release a nasty venom which causes more pain than a bee sting – OUCH!

Saddleback caterpillars don't always look so impressive, though. When the tiny caterpillars hatch from their eggs, they don't have lime green sides or long spikes, instead they are small, pale, and squishy. It is only after they shed their skin a few times that they gain their bold green patterns and sharp spines. And when the caterpillars undergo their final costume change during metamorphosis, they lose their fancy outfit and emerge as small, brown moths.

With spiky horns at the front and back, it's hard to tell which end of the saddleback caterpillar is which!

Australian horror moth caterpillars
feast on poisonous leaves.

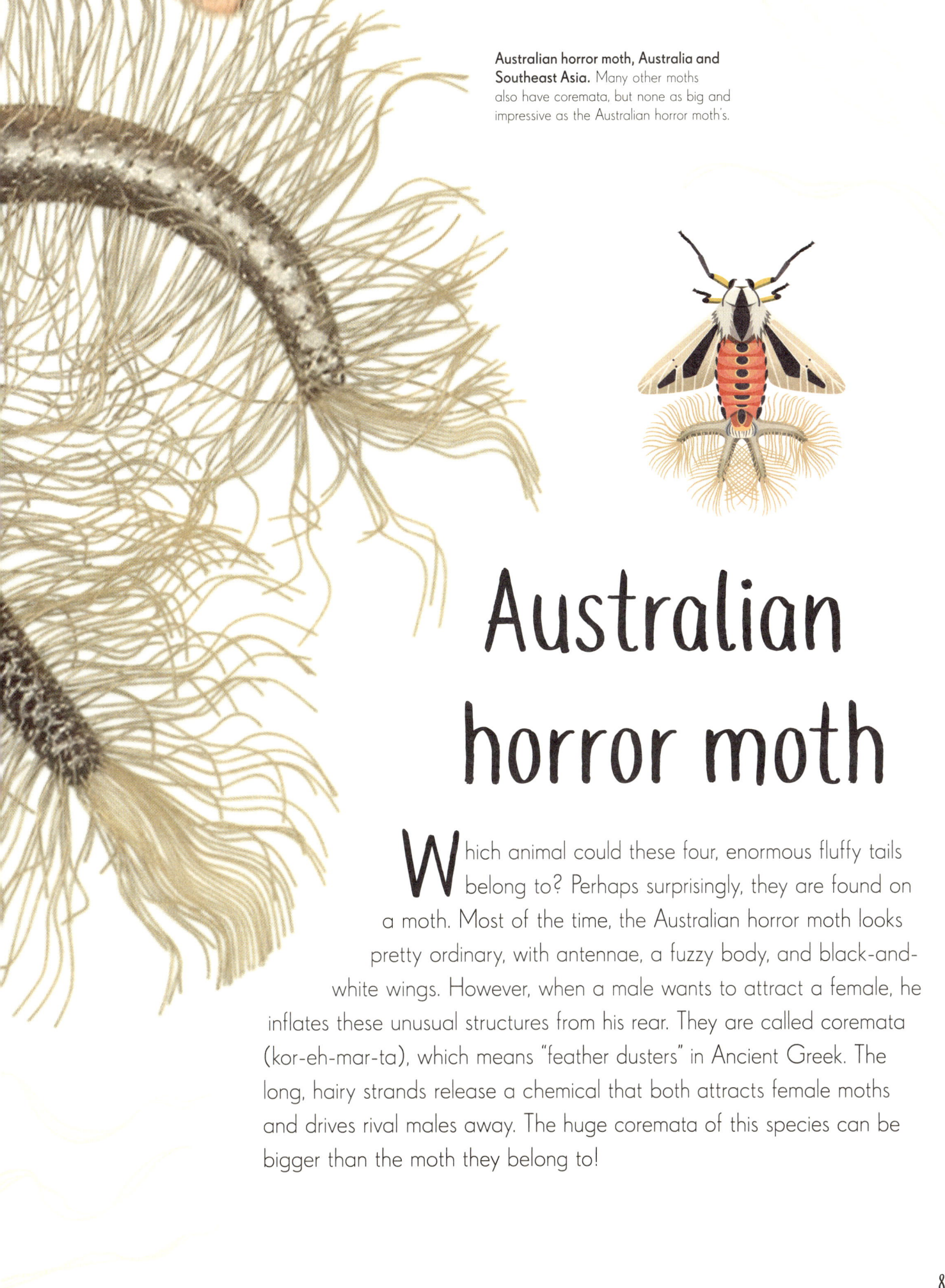

Australian horror moth, Australia and Southeast Asia. Many other moths also have coremata, but none as big and impressive as the Australian horror moth's.

Australian horror moth

Which animal could these four, enormous fluffy tails belong to? Perhaps surprisingly, they are found on a moth. Most of the time, the Australian horror moth looks pretty ordinary, with antennae, a fuzzy body, and black-and-white wings. However, when a male wants to attract a female, he inflates these unusual structures from his rear. They are called coremata (kor-eh-mar-ta), which means "feather dusters" in Ancient Greek. The long, hairy strands release a chemical that both attracts female moths and drives rival males away. The huge coremata of this species can be bigger than the moth they belong to!

Asian dune cricket

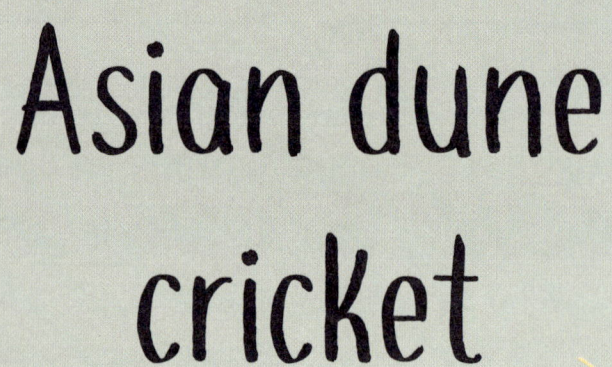

Life in the desert is hard. It's hot and dry, and there's not a lot to eat, so the animals that live there must be tough and resourceful. Dune crickets are no exception. Working alone, they use their powerful mouthparts to dig burrows in the sand, kicking the grains away with their large feet and only stopping when they dig deep enough to find ground that is wet. During the day, they rest in these tunnels, plugged at the entrance with sand to keep them safe from the scorching heat of the sun. Then, after dark, they pop out to hunt. They are not fussy eaters and will gobble up anything from beetles and grasshoppers to other crickets and small frogs.

The burrows dug by dune crickets can be more than 1 m (3 ft) long!

Asian dune cricket, southern Asia.
Also known as splay-footed crickets, these insects have long "toes" that stop them sinking into the sand.

Some groups of cicadas spend 17 years underground, while others only wait 13 years.

Pharaoh cicada, North America. When adult cicadas first emerge from their old exoskeleton, their body is pale and soft. After about an hour they become much darker.

Pharaoh cicada

Imagine spending the first 17 years of your life underground, never seeing the sun — that's exactly what pharaoh cicadas do. Once they have hatched from eggs in the soil, young cicadas burrow towards tree roots and slurp their sap. Over many years, they slowly grow bigger. Finally, one night, when conditions are just right, they clamber up onto the surface, all at the same time. Thousands of them may emerge on the same evening! The young cicadas then march towards the nearest tree, climb to the upper branches and begin to moult a final time. After nearly two decades, the winged adults finally emerge. However, they will only live for a month before laying their eggs and dying, then the cycle starts again.

Wheel bug

Wheel bugs get their name from the impressive cog-like structure on their back.

Wheel bugs belong to a group of insects known as assassin bugs, and if you saw one, it would soon be clear why. A wheel bug stabs its insect prey with a long beak and injects a special saliva that turns its target's insides into liquid. Then it slurps up the grisly soup through its straw-like mouthparts! Using this method, it gobbles up caterpillars, beetles, stink bugs, and other small insects.

As well as their sharp beak, wheel bugs have strong front legs, which can be used for grabbing hold of their prey. When they are frightened, female wheel bugs pop out bright orange glands from the end of their body and release a foul smell to frighten off predators.

Wheel bug, South America.
Wheel bugs are active in the daytime, but they are large and slow-moving insects.

Southern flannel moth

Southern flannel moth caterpillars grow into moths that are just as fluffy.

So cute and fluffy… If you spotted the southern flannel moth caterpillar on a leaf, there's a good chance you wouldn't realize it was an insect. You might even want to pick it up and give it a cuddle. But don't do that! This is one of the most venomous caterpillars on the planet. Those soft and downy hairs hide sharp spines loaded with toxins which can make you very sick. As well as causing pain and itching to the skin, the venom of this insect can cause fever, headaches, vomiting, and worse. These caterpillars have even caused schools to close, when children were stung by them.

Southern flannel moth, eastern North America. Southern flannel moth caterpillars get hairier each time they moult.

European hornet

Hornets have large, C-shaped eyes that they use to hunt their prey.

Buzzing through the air like striped fighter jets, European hornets might seem ferocious. They are loud, large, and their bright colours shout "DANGER!". But their sting is actually less toxic than that of a honeybee, and they are less likely to use it. Compared to their paper wasp cousins, hornets are very calm. Although they can sting again and again if they need to, they will only do so if they think their nest or colony is at risk.

European hornets build impressive nests made of chewed-up wood pulp. These beautiful, banded structures look very delicate, but are strong enough to protect the queen, her young, and the rest of the colony from predators and extreme weather.

European hornet, Asia and Europe.
Hornets use their powerful jaws, with many moving parts, to eat their prey or chew up wood.

Long-horned orb weaver

Female long-horned orb weavers have much longer spines than males.

Long-horned orb weaver, Asia.
Long-horned orb weavers are about as wide as your little finger.

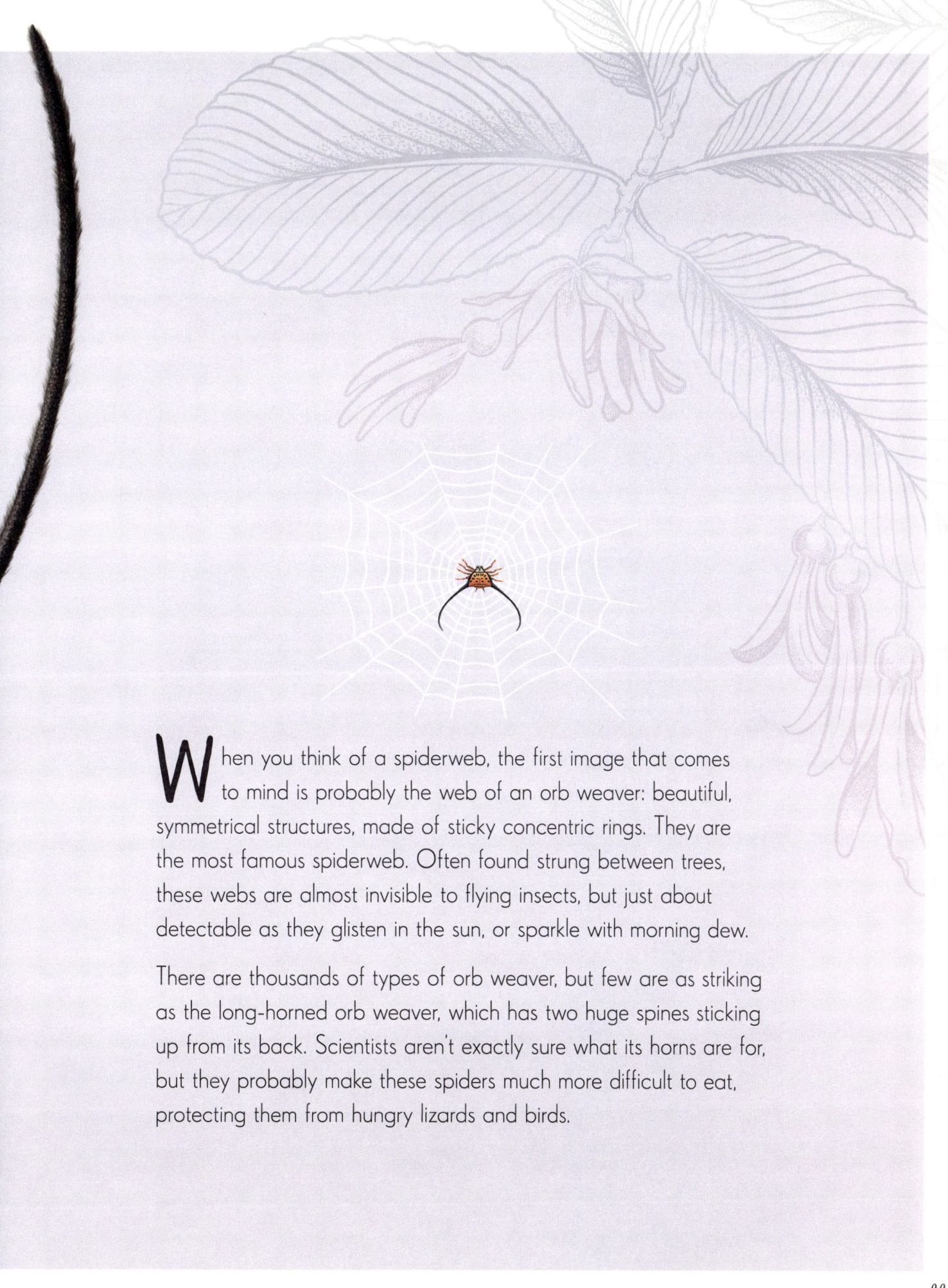

When you think of a spiderweb, the first image that comes to mind is probably the web of an orb weaver: beautiful, symmetrical structures, made of sticky concentric rings. They are the most famous spiderweb. Often found strung between trees, these webs are almost invisible to flying insects, but just about detectable as they glisten in the sun, or sparkle with morning dew.

There are thousands of types of orb weaver, but few are as striking as the long-horned orb weaver, which has two huge spines sticking up from its back. Scientists aren't exactly sure what its horns are for, but they probably make these spiders much more difficult to eat, protecting them from hungry lizards and birds.

Brown-lipped snail

Spirals are common in nature. They can be found in flowers, pine cones, and even galaxies. Almost all snail shells have spirals, though they come in many different shapes and sizes. Sometimes, even snails of the same species can display a variety of colours. The shell of a brown-lipped snail may be yellow, brown, orange, or pink, but they always have a dark brown band around the opening.

When the weather is damp, brown-lipped snails can be found gliding through the undergrowth on glistening trails of slime. But when the weather turns hot and dry, they retreat into their shell and seal up the entrance, to prevent themselves from losing too much moisture.

A snail is born with its shell, but the number of spirals increases as it grows!

Brown-lipped snail, Europe.
These snails often have beautiful bands that make a spiral pattern around their shell.

Giant frog-legged beetle

From a quick glance at a male frog-legged beetle, with its chunky thighs, you might think that its jumps could rival those of a frog. In fact, unlike their namesakes, frog-legged beetles don't jump at all. They get around by walking or flying — and flying is made more difficult by the weight of their legs. So, what is the point of those huge hindlegs? The answer is that they are used for wrestling! Rival males will battle one another to impress females, using their powerful legs to push and shove each other out of the way. Female frog-legged beetles, which don't fight, have legs that are significantly more slender.

Frog-legged beetles are also known as
"kangaroo beetles" because of the
shape of their legs.

Giant frog-legged beetle, Southeast Asia. The metallic wing cases of the giant frog-legged beetle protect its delicate wings, which are folded up when not in use.

African giant flower beetle, central Africa. There have been over 80 colour variations of African flower beetles found!

Hercules beetle, Central America. The male hercules beetle has a long horn that it uses to battle other males.

Glorious scarab, southern North America. Adult glorious scarabs love to nibble juniper trees, but their larvae prefer rotting wood.

Scarab beetles

Goliath beetle, Africa. The goliath beetle is one of the world's largest beetles, and one of the heaviest insects.

Common cockchafer, Europe. The common cockchafer is easily identified by its amazing feathery antennae.

Sun beetle, central and western Africa. Sun beetles survive on a diet of plants, and ripe and rotten fruit.

Glittering flower beetle, central Africa. Male glittering flower beetles have a T-shaped horn on their head.

When people think of scarab beetles, they may think of ancient Egypt, where these insects were famously depicted rolling the sun across the sky. But the scarab family stretches much further than the deserts of northern Africa. In fact, there are more than 30,000 species of scarab beetle! Many of them live in tropical forests, but they can be found all over the planet, in lots of different environments. Some are important pollinators, and others clear up waste — most famously the dung beetles.

Scarab beetles usually have tough, oval-shaped exoskeletons, many of which glitter and shimmer with brilliant colours.

Spring dumbledor, western Asia and Europe. Spring dumbledors usually look black, but have a beautiful iridescent shine in the sun.

Spotted-wing antlion

Imagine you're an ant, hurrying back to your nest, when suddenly the ground crumbles beneath your feet! You tumble down the steep slopes of a funnel-shaped trap, straight towards a hungry antlion larva. Luckily, you manage to dodge its snapping jaws, and start to scramble back up the edges of the pit… but the cunning larva then showers you with sand to knock you back down and grab you.

Antlion larvae are very patient. Once they have made their trap, they may wait days or weeks, buried up to their jaws, for a meal to drop by. They can live like this for some years, before eventually transforming into a winged adult that looks a little like a damselfly.

Antlion larvae are sometimes called doodlebugs because of the winding trails they leave behind them in the sand.

Larva

Adult

Spotted wing antlion, northern Africa, western Asia, and Europe. Antlion larvae use their powerful jaws to grasp and pierce the exoskeleton of their prey.

The wasp mantidfly looks like a combination of a wasp and a praying mantis — but it is neither!

Wasp mantidfly

Something striped zooms past and lands on a leaf. Its colours remind you of a wasp, but its arms are tucked in front of it like a praying mantis. What is this mysterious creature? It's a wasp mantidfly! Despite its name, this bug is more closely related to lacewings than any other insect. Mantidflies do not have a stinger, but they do an excellent job of dressing up to make themselves look scary. Their colourful stripes trick larger animals into thinking they are stinging wasps, making any predator pause before trying to eat them. Strong, spiky front legs are used just like a mantis's to catch smaller insects to eat, but mantidflies also enjoy sugary nectar.

Wasp mantidfly, North America. Mantidflies hold their spiky front legs folded underneath their head, just like a praying mantis.

Shocking pink dragon millipede

Although it is less than 3 cm (1 in) long — around half the length of your little finger — you wouldn't miss the shocking pink dragon millipede! It is the brightest, most flamboyant member of the millipede family. With a pink exoskeleton and a train of spines along its back, this is a millipede that is happy to be seen. Like many of the world's most vibrant creatures, its bright colour means "Watch out, I'm poisonous!". If a predator comes too close, this millipede oozes a toxic liquid from the sides of its body. Despite its eye-catching wardrobe, the shocking pink dragon millipede was first described by scientists in 2007, perhaps because it lives inside caverns.

Although it has a delicious scent of almonds,
the poison of the dragon millipede can be deadly.

**Shocking pink dragon millipede,
Thailand.** The shocking pink dragon
millipede has around 60 long, pink legs.
Unlike centipedes, millipedes have two
legs on each side of a body segment.

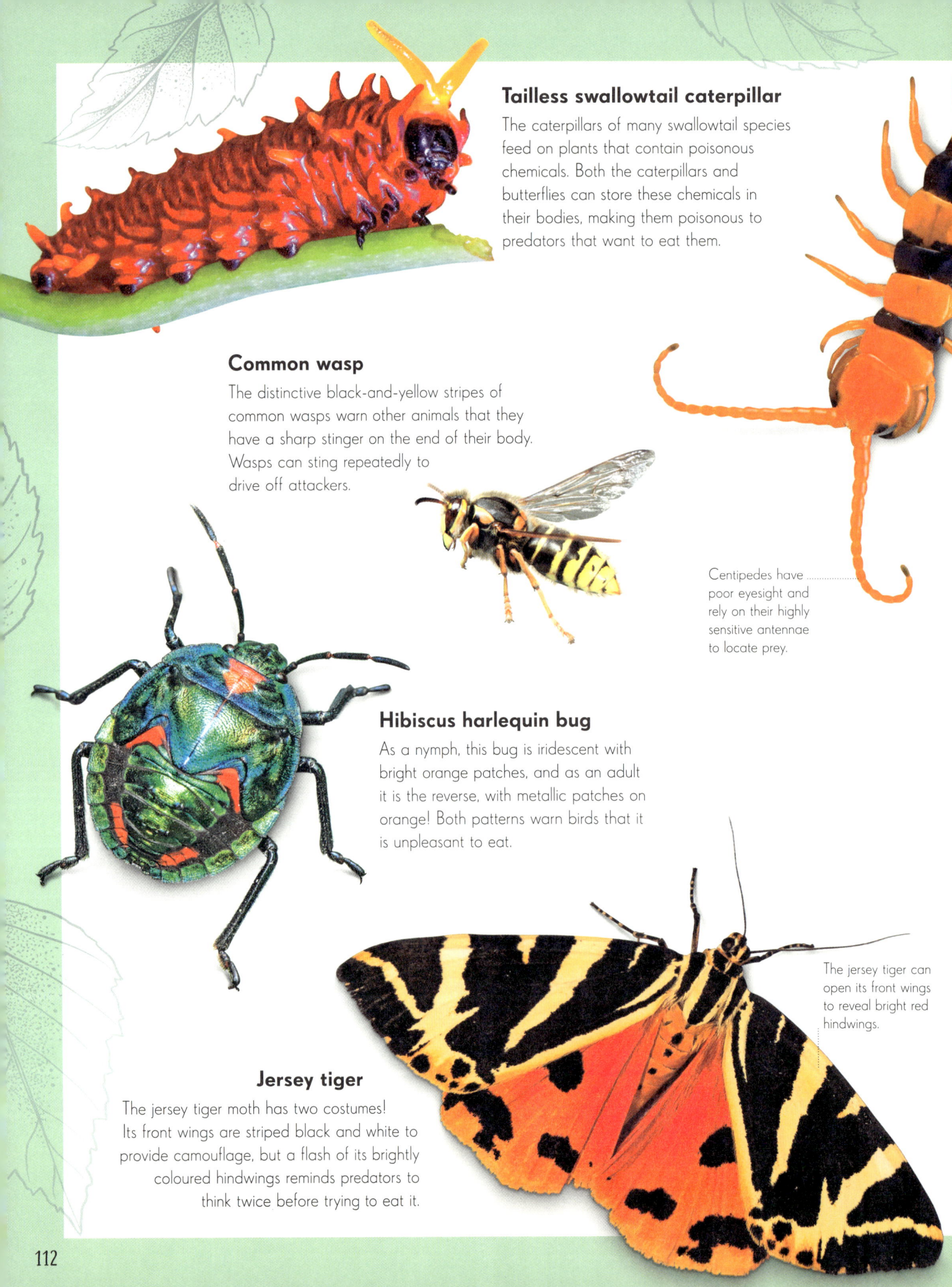

Tailless swallowtail caterpillar

The caterpillars of many swallowtail species feed on plants that contain poisonous chemicals. Both the caterpillars and butterflies can store these chemicals in their bodies, making them poisonous to predators that want to eat them.

Common wasp

The distinctive black-and-yellow stripes of common wasps warn other animals that they have a sharp stinger on the end of their body. Wasps can sting repeatedly to drive off attackers.

Centipedes have poor eyesight and rely on their highly sensitive antennae to locate prey.

Hibiscus harlequin bug

As a nymph, this bug is iridescent with bright orange patches, and as an adult it is the reverse, with metallic patches on orange! Both patterns warn birds that it is unpleasant to eat.

The jersey tiger can open its front wings to reveal bright red hindwings.

Jersey tiger

The jersey tiger moth has two costumes! Its front wings are striped black and white to provide camouflage, but a flash of its brightly coloured hindwings reminds predators to think twice before trying to eat it.

Hawaiian happy face spider

These colourful spiders usually hide underneath leaves, but their next defence is their bright colours. They come in a variety of patterns, usually featuring red, black, and white on a yellow background.

Sometimes, the patterning on the back of this spider can look like a smiley face!

Indian tiger centipede

These super speedy bugs are striped orange and black like a tiger, and they are also deadly hunters. They deliver their powerful venom through super sharp claws — perfect for piercing through skin.

Warning colours

Most bugs try to go about unseen by predators, but some wear bright, bold colours to make sure that they will be spotted. This may seem like a bad idea, but these colours are a warning. They mean "Don't eat me, I'm poisonous!", or "Watch out! I have a nasty sting!". The most common warning colours in the animal kingdom are yellow, orange, and red, sometimes combined with black spots and stripes. If a predator has a bad experience when trying to eat one brightly-coloured animal, it may be put off attacking anything that colour for the rest of its life! Scientists call this special defence strategy "aposematism".

Western horse lubber grasshopper

Using chemicals collected from the plants that it eats, the western horse lubber grasshopper produces its own toxic poison. It releases this as a foam when it feels threatened.

Giant robber fly

A robber fly perches on a leaf, silently waiting for its prey to pass by. You might not see it, but it definitely sees you! With large eyes, robber flies have excellent vision and are constantly scanning their surroundings. The moment a potential meal moves into range, the robber fly springs into action with the deadly precision of an aerial assassin.

Catching insects while mid-flight is the robber fly's speciality. It locks onto its target and agile wings quickly propel it forwards. Then, it uses its long, bristly legs to reach out and snatch prey right out of the air. Robber flies are not fussy. Grasshoppers, dragonflies, butterflies, beetles, bees, and wasps are all on the menu for these fearsome predators.

A fuzzy "moustache" of hair on
a robber fly's face protects it
from other insects.

Giant robber fly, southern Africa.
Robber flies have a sharp proboscis
that pierces through the exoskeleton
of other insects and injects
toxic saliva.

Violet oil beetle

Oil beetles have huge, black bodies, which shimmer violet-blue in the sunlight. But they don't always look so handsome. When young, oil beetle larvae are known as triungulins. They are smaller than ants and look a bit like tiny earwigs. As soon as they hatch, triungulins shimmy to the very top of the nearest flower, and wait. When a solitary bee lands to gather nectar, a triungulin hops onto its back and rides all the way back to the bee's nest. Once there, the baby beetle gobbles up the bee's eggs and pollen stores! Then, it settles down to transform. Next year, it will emerge as an adult and start the cycle again.

Violet oil beetle, northern Africa, western Asia, and Europe. Adult oil beetles have large bodies and tiny wing cases, so it is impossible for them to fly.

Triungulin

Adult

Oil beetles produce one of the most toxic chemicals in the world!

Bullet ant, Central America and South America. Bullet ants can use their sharp, pointed stingers to sting again and again.

Bullet ant

Ouch! The bullet ant has the most painful sting of any animal on the planet. Its stinger is not much longer than a grain of sand, but packs a punch as powerful as a bullet from a gun — and the pain can last for up to 24 hours! Bullet ants live in the tropical rainforests of Central and South America. They build their nests underground at the base of trees and the workers can often be seen patrolling towering trunks and sky-high branches in search of nectar and other insects to eat. If they feel threatened, bullet ants will usually use their pincer-like mouthparts to fight back first, only resorting to their potent sting if that doesn't work.

Growing up to 3 cm (1 in) long, bullet ants are big! However, unlike many other ant species, the queen is roughly the same size as the workers.

Black and yellow mud dauber

A single mud dauber can build a nest as big as a lemon.

A muddy puddle shines in the afternoon sun. At the edge of the water, a shape darts purposefully along the water's edge. Look closer, and you will see that it is a slender, black-and-yellow wasp with its head down, gathering mud in its jaws. The black and yellow mud dauber carefully shapes a ball of wet clay and then flies off to find a sheltered spot to start building. It presses the ball of mud into place, then returns to the puddle to gather more. Eventually, it forms a collection of long tubes stuck together. What are they for though? The wasp fills them with paralysed spiders and then lays an egg in each tube. The unlucky bugs will feed the young when they hatch!

Black and yellow mud dauber, North America. The black and yellow mud dauber carefully shapes mud into a round ball.

Male

Female

Striped scorpionfly

Scorpionflies are sneaky scavengers and sometimes steal dead insects from spiderwebs.

Striped scorpionfly, North America.
Scorpionflies have long beaks that they use to munch on dead plants and animals.

The long, coiled tail of male scorpionflies and their striking black and yellow colouring makes them look quite frightening, doesn't it? But do not fear, there's no sting here! Scorpionflies are harmless to people and animals. In place of the sting you would find at the end of a scorpion's tail, the male scorpionfly has special organs for mating.

Though they look a bit like craneflies, scorpionflies are actually more closely related to fleas. They are not fussy eaters, feasting on whatever they can find, from rotting plants and animals to pollen and nectar. Their vibrant colouring tricks predators into thinking they are more dangerous than they really are.

Male

Female

Giraffe weevil

Giraffe weevil, Madagascar. Male giraffe weevils use their long necks to fight each other.

What a long neck! This odd-looking beetle lives in the forests of Madagascar, so is its neck used to reach leaves like a giraffe's? No. Males use their supersize necks for fighting each other, in the hope of attracting a female. The female weevil's neck is much shorter than the male's, and she does not fight. She is a master builder! By carefully nipping, bending, and folding a soft leaf from her favourite tree, she uses her strong legs to create a protective roll in which to lay her egg. Once she is finished, she snips the leaf roll from the stem, where it falls to the forest floor, keeping her egg safe from predators until it hatches.

The male giraffe weevil's neck is about twice as long as the female's neck.

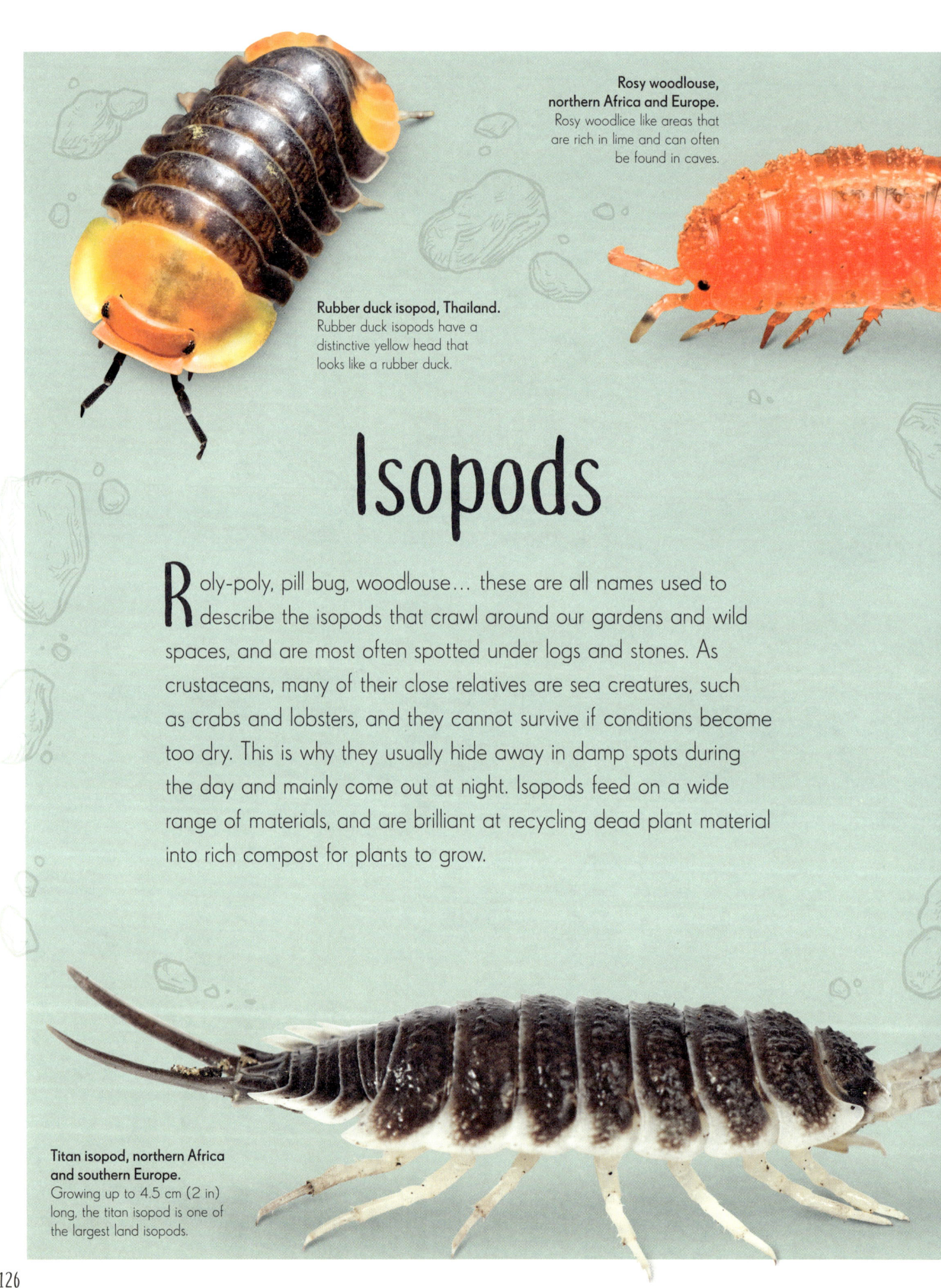

Rosy woodlouse, northern Africa and Europe.
Rosy woodlice like areas that are rich in lime and can often be found in caves.

Rubber duck isopod, Thailand.
Rubber duck isopods have a distinctive yellow head that looks like a rubber duck.

Isopods

Roly-poly, pill bug, woodlouse… these are all names used to describe the isopods that crawl around our gardens and wild spaces, and are most often spotted under logs and stones. As crustaceans, many of their close relatives are sea creatures, such as crabs and lobsters, and they cannot survive if conditions become too dry. This is why they usually hide away in damp spots during the day and mainly come out at night. Isopods feed on a wide range of materials, and are brilliant at recycling dead plant material into rich compost for plants to grow.

Titan isopod, northern Africa and southern Europe.
Growing up to 4.5 cm (2 in) long, the titan isopod is one of the largest land isopods.

Dairy cow isopod, northern Africa.
Like all isopods, the dairy cow isopod
has seven main body segments —
each with its own pair of legs.

Of the 10,000 species of
isopod that we know of,
around half live in water.

Granulated isopod, Spain.
Granulated isopods can roll into a
ball when they feel threatened.

Silverfish

Whut's that glint in the corner? Small, scaly silverfish love sheltered places. In the wild, they might be found in dusty, hollow tree trunks or under old logs, but they are also very attracted to the dark parts of human homes. Their small size allows them to squeeze their way through tiny cracks in the walls of houses and to find their way into bathrooms, basements, and attics, where they come out at night to scout around for food. Silverfish are harmless to humans, though they can trigger allergies, but they do have an inconvenient habit of nibbling on our belongings. As well as feasting on human food, they have also been known to gobble soap, hair, dust, glue, clothes, and books!

Silverfish are one of the most ancient types of insect, and are around 400 million years old.

Silverfish, worldwide, except the Arctic and Antarctic. This image shows a silverfish's eye. It is made up of many small, round parts called ommatidia.

Common glowworm, Asia and Europe.
The chemical reaction that creates light happens in an organ at the end of the glowworm's body.

Despite their name,
glowworms are actually
a type of beetle.

Male

Female

Common glowworm

It's not surprising that in the past, the sight of fields of glimmering glowworms sparked stories of fairies carrying tiny lanterns. But the "magic" of a glowworm's twinkling light is actually created by a chemical reaction within its body, which produces a bright, cold glow.

Female glowworms have large, bulky bodies and no wings, but they shine the brightest. Males are smaller but do have wings, which allows them to fly above the grass, scanning the stems for a glowing mate. Adult glowworms don't eat, so only survive for a few weeks. This gives them just enough time to mate and lay eggs. Adult glowworms, their larvae, and even their eggs can glow!

Giant strong-nosed stink bug, southern North America and northern South America. The black-and-red stink bug nymphs have a rounder body than the shield-shaped adults.

Stink bugs are also known as shield bugs, because of their broad, flat bodies.

Giant strong-nosed stink bug

Stink bugs have sharp, pointed mouthparts, but they aren't usually dangerous. Most simply pierce leaves, vegetables, and fruits to get at the sweet sap inside, but giant strong-nosed stink bugs are in fact predators — and they're particularly fond of caterpillars. Both the camouflaged adults and their brightly-coloured nymphs love to feast on the juices inside other insects.

While many types of stink bug are seen as pests because of the damage they do to plants, giant strong-nosed stink bugs are actually favoured by gardeners and farmers because they gobble up animals that would otherwise damage crops. When they feel scared or threatened, stink bugs can release a cloud of foul-smelling gas, to make their attacker think twice about getting any closer.

Torreya trapdoor spider

A thick round disc on its rear protects
this small spider from predators.

Torreya trapdoor spider, eastern North America. These spiders build burrows on sloping river banks and ravines.

Imagine watching a beetle walk along the ground when suddenly a little door opens and the beetle is pulled inside! This is the home of a trapdoor spider. These spiders live in silk-lined burrows with hinged doors at the entrance, disguised with soil and plants. When lunch walks by, vibrations alert the trapdoor spider and it flings open the door and ambushes its prey with remarkable speed.

The Torreya trapdoor spider's burrow also protects it from predators. The tunnel is built to be the perfect size for its round, shield-like rear to fit tightly inside the walls. When threatened, the spider retreats inside, scuttling head-first into its home, plugging the burrow and making it almost impossible to extract.

Blue carpenter bee

Buzzing through the air in tropical woodlands, these bees look and sound like tiny blue helicopters!

Blue carpenter bee, southern Asia and Southeast Asia. These bees have blue hair on their head and the front part of their body.

Blue is a relatively rare colour in the natural world, so blue animals are always very striking – and the female blue carpenter bee is no exception. Her chunky blue body ends in a sharp stinger, but she is not aggressive and would much prefer not to use it. The males are less brightly coloured with green or brown hair.

Unlike honeybees and bumblebees, which live in large groups, carpenter bees live alone. As their name suggests, they like to make things from wood! They chew tunnels in trees into which they lay their eggs. Though they don't care for their young in the same way honeybees do, they make sure to leave them a parcel of food before sealing the tunnel.

Grasshoppers

Although they are famous for their extraordinary leaping abilities, most grasshoppers are also brilliant fliers!

Horsehead grasshopper, South America. Horsehead grasshoppers are so well camouflaged as twigs that they are often confused with stick insects, and sticks!

Elegant grasshopper, Africa. The striking colours of the elegant grasshopper tell predators that it is poisonous to eat.

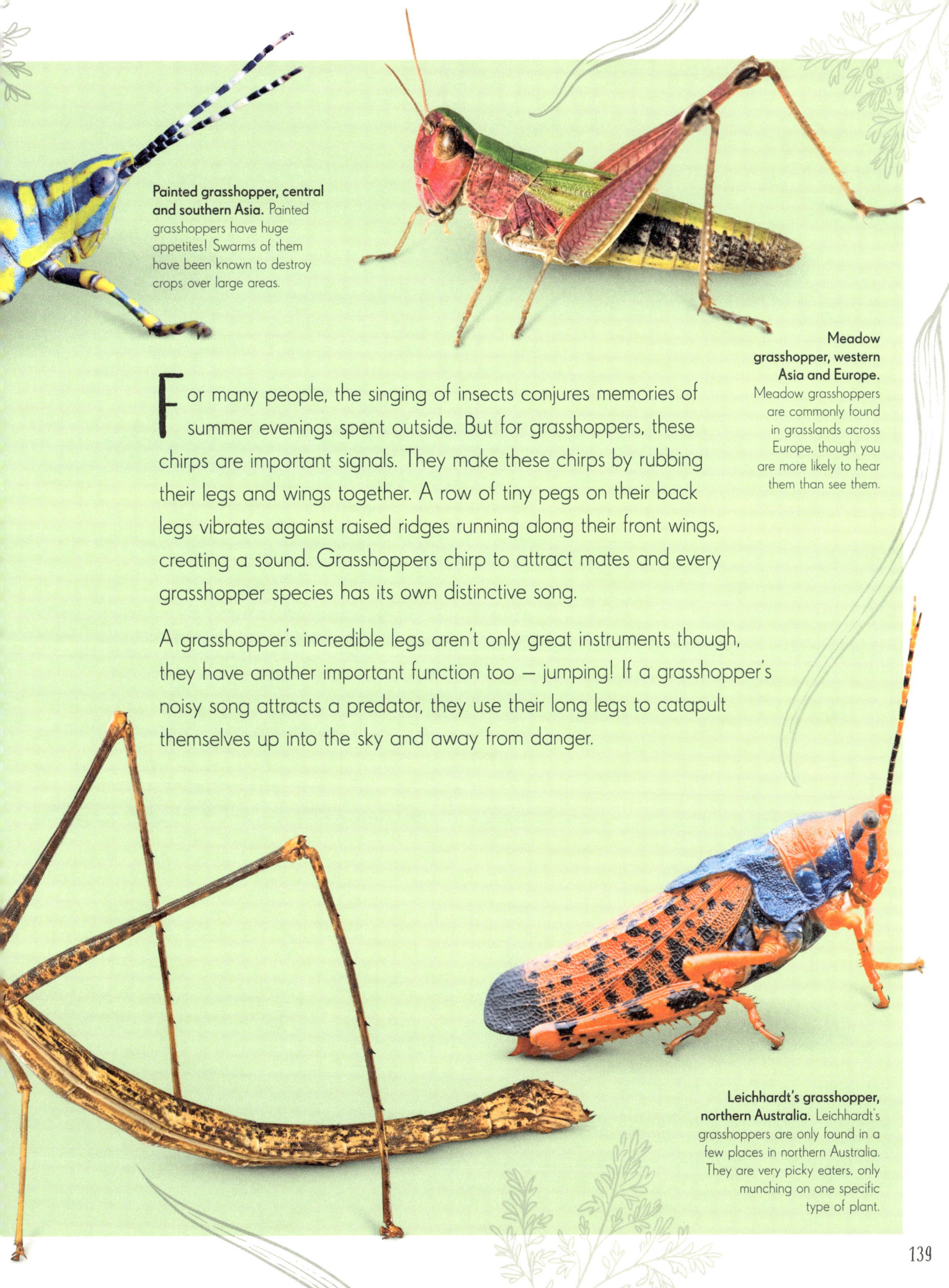

Painted grasshopper, central and southern Asia. Painted grasshoppers have huge appetites! Swarms of them have been known to destroy crops over large areas.

Meadow grasshopper, western Asia and Europe. Meadow grasshoppers are commonly found in grasslands across Europe, though you are more likely to hear them than see them.

For many people, the singing of insects conjures memories of summer evenings spent outside. But for grasshoppers, these chirps are important signals. They make these chirps by rubbing their legs and wings together. A row of tiny pegs on their back legs vibrates against raised ridges running along their front wings, creating a sound. Grasshoppers chirp to attract mates and every grasshopper species has its own distinctive song.

A grasshopper's incredible legs aren't only great instruments though, they have another important function too — jumping! If a grasshopper's noisy song attracts a predator, they use their long legs to catapult themselves up into the sky and away from danger.

Leichhardt's grasshopper, northern Australia. Leichhardt's grasshoppers are only found in a few places in northern Australia. They are very picky eaters, only munching on one specific type of plant.

Golden-bloomed grey longhorn beetle

Is this a cuddly toy? Golden-bloomed grey longhorn beetles certainly look like they would be perfect to snuggle, with their cosy coat of fuzzy, golden hairs. But in reality, they are not all that cuddly! They have hard wing cases to protect their soft wings, and chomping mouthparts for munching holes in tough plants such as thistles.

Why do these insects have such long antennae, though? Their supersize feelers are covered in sensors that help them seek out mates and plants. A female lays a single egg inside her chosen plant. Once the larva hatches, it mines its way down the stem to near ground level. There it makes a pupa and snoozes through the winter, emerging in the spring as an adult.

There are more than 35,000 species of longhorn beetle found all over the world.

Golden-bloomed grey longhorn beetle, western Asia and Europe. The golden-bloomed grey longhorn beetle's stripy antennae can be longer than its body.

Japanese giant water bug

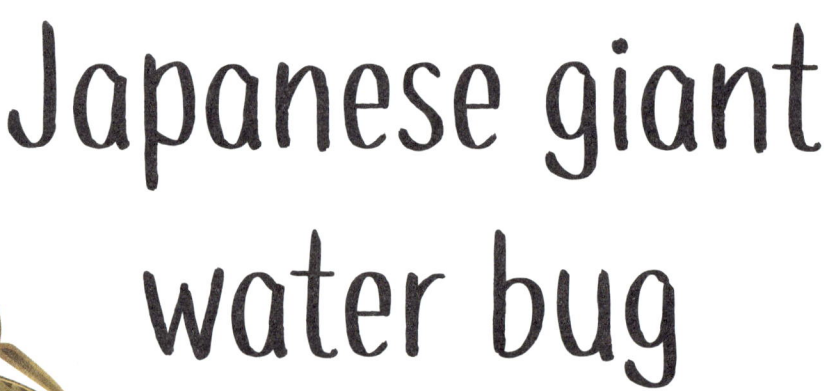

Known in some parts of the world as "toebiters", giant water bugs can sometimes nip the feet of human bathers!

Japanese giant water bug, eastern Asia. The eggs on the back of this male Japanese giant water bug have started to hatch.

Lurking at the bottom of ponds, lakes, and slow-moving rivers across the world, giant water bugs bide their time, waiting — perfectly still — for the perfect moment to pounce. When a tadpole, frog, or other small water creature moves into the strike zone, the giant water bug leaps to action, snatching its prey using its powerful front legs. It grips its victim tightly before piercing it with its sharp, dagger-like mouthparts.

Unusually for insects, male giant water bugs are caring fathers. Females lay their eggs on the male's back, then he carries the brood with him everywhere he goes until they hatch. He protects them from predators and makes sure they get enough oxygen by routinely bringing them to the water's surface.

Some stick insect eggs have a cap that attracts ants. The ants take the eggs back to their nest where they will be safe.

Indian stick insect

Like leaf insects, stick insects lay hard-shelled eggs that often resemble seeds. The eggs have a "door" at one end, through which the baby stick insect emerges.

Common house mosquito

Mosquitoes lay rafts of eggs that float on the surface of still water. Many flying insects lay their eggs on or near water because their larvae are aquatic and can swim as soon as they hatch.

Eggs

Almost all invertebrates begin their life inside an egg. This is usually a hard structure, with a strong shell to protect it from drying out or being attacked by predators. But the range of colours and shapes of bug eggs is enormous. Sometimes, eggs are laid alone, but more often they are laid in clusters. It's important that eggs are laid somewhere they will be safe from harm, as most bugs do not stay with their eggs after laying them. Eggs are also usually left near — or on — a source of food, so that the young can start eating as soon as they hatch!

The surface of these eggs becomes sticky when wet.

Philippine leaf insect

Leaf insects let their eggs drop to the forest floor. At first, the eggs look smooth, but their surface soon hardens to form impressive spikes, which are thought to mimic the appearance of seeds.

Harlequin cabbage bug

Harlequin cabbage bugs lay their eggs in clusters of around fourteen, usually attached to the bottom of a leaf. When the young bugs hatch, they start to feed immediately.

These eggs have bold black and white patterns but the larvae inside are orange and black.

Kissing bug

Female kissing bugs feed on blood to get the energy to produce their eggs. They can lay up to 40 eggs after a meal and glue the eggs securely in places where the larvae will be able to find a host to bite!

Map butterfly

Map butterflies lay their eggs in strings, which they hang from the leaves of stinging nettles — the favoured food of their caterpillars. The adults have different wing patterns depending on if they hatched from their eggs in the spring or the summer.

Black cockroach

Cockroaches and praying mantises lay their eggs within a protective structure called an ootheca (oo-thee-ka). Within the ootheca there are many long eggs lined up next to each other that will all hatch at the same time.

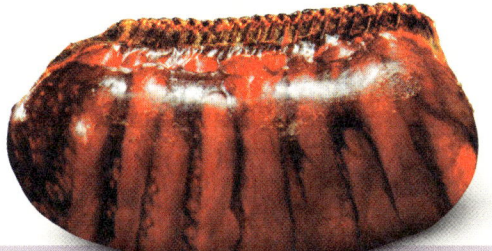

Seven-spot ladybird

Ladybirds attach groups of their small, shiny, yellow eggs to the leaves and stems of plants where there are plenty of aphids for their young to eat. The newly hatched larvae are born ready to hunt.

Common green lacewing

The network of green veins on a lacewing's
wings look like fine lace fabric.

As daylight fades, common green lacewings take to the air. Their delicate wings are covered in intricate veins, which sparkle in the moonlight as the insects flutter gracefully through the sky. Lacewings are drawn to sweet foods, such as nectar, and use their long antennae to seek out the tastiest flowers.

To attract a mate, lacewings shake their bodies very fast, sending vibrations through the leaves they are standing on. Other lacewings hear these sounds using ears found at the base of their wings! Female lacewings lay their small eggs on long stalks, which keeps them safe from predators. This includes other lacewing larvae, which have large jaws for munching on aphids and other small insects.

Namib desert beetle, southern Africa. Namib desert beetles position themselves at the peak of sand dunes to collect the most fog.

These beetles sometimes bury themselves beneath the sand to hide from the scorching sun.

Namib desert beetle

For some animals, finding water is easy. But for Namib desert beetles, which live in one of the hottest, driest places on the planet, getting a drink is not so simple. Very little rain falls in the Namib desert. Instead, most water comes in the form of fog from the sea. When fog rolls in, clever Namib desert beetles scuttle to the top of the sand dunes where the fog is densest and position themselves, head down, into the wind. Water droplets soon form on their wing cases and trickle down special grooves, directly into their mouths. This amazing behaviour is known as "fog-basking" and allows the ingenious beetles to survive.

European honeybee, worldwide, except the Arctic and Antarctic.
Up to 80,000 bees can live in a hive. Most of the bees are workers. There is usually only a single queen and a few hundred drones.

European honeybee

Worker bees are all daughters of the queen, making them sisters!

Queen

Drone

Worker

Buzz... Buzz... There's no busier sound in the world than the hum of a bustling honeybee hive. And a good job too, there's lots of work to be done! Every worker bee has a role to play, be it searching for food, defending the hive, caring for the queen and her young, or keeping their home clean and tidy. There is also the queen, who lays eggs, and male drones, whose only role is to mate with new queens. It's not just about working hard though, it's about working together. When foragers return to the hive, laden with pollen and nectar, they dance to tell the other workers where the best flowers can be found.

Wheel spider

A wheel spider can spin
44 times in just one second!

Have you ever seen a cartwheeling spider? Wheel spiders tuck in their legs and fling themselves down sand dunes to escape from danger. And, in the Namib desert, danger lurks around every corner. The wheel spider's archenemy, the pompilid wasp, is always on the hunt for new wheel spiders to feed to her babies. Although wheel spiders hunt at night and spend their days tucked up in deep sand burrows, pompilid wasps are relentless. They will dig out wheel spiders, even if they are hidden far beneath the surface. Once the spider is uncovered, running is impossible, so it relies on its gymnastic moves to spin itself to safety!

Wheel spider, southern Africa. Wheel spiders have large fangs which they use to grab insects and other bite-sized bugs.

Gold-necked carrion beetle

A carrion beetle's club-like antennae are used to pick up the faintest smell of a dead animal.

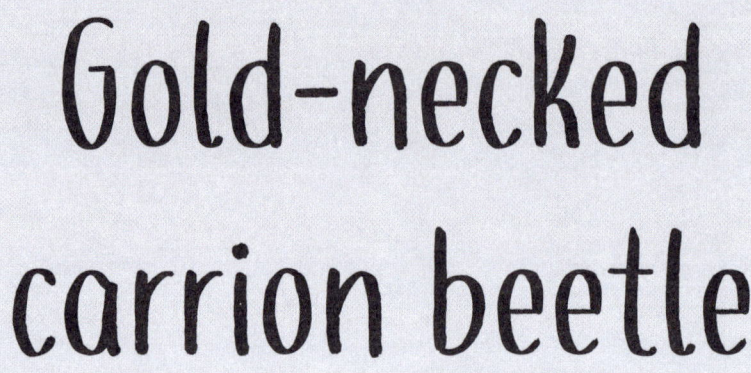

Gold-necked carrion beetle, North America. The bright colours on its back tell predators that this carrion beetle is not good to eat.

Most insects lay their eggs and then disappear, leaving their young to fend for themselves — but not carrion beetles. To give their larvae the best possible start, gold-necked carrion beetles first use their highly sensitive antennae to sniff out a dead animal. Once they have located one, the parent beetles excavate the soil under it, so it falls into a hole to hide it from other scavengers. They also remove any inedible hair or feathers. When the larvae hatch, they tuck in straight away to this gruesome feast!

Their habit of burying dead animals makes carrion beetles brilliant recyclers. The nutrients inside the carcass are eaten by their larvae or released back into the soil, which helps plants to grow.

Yellow-horned velvet ant, South America. Velvet ants, including the yellow-horned velvet ant, have extremely strong exoskeletons.

Velvet ants

Female

Male

Pacific velvet ant, western North America. The bright colours of the Pacific velvet ant warn predators to stay away.

Thistledown velvet ant, southern North America. The thistledown velvet ant lays its eggs in the nests of sand wasps.

Red velvet ant, southern North America. Also known as the "cow killer", the red velvet ant has a very painful sting.

Female velvet ants may look fluffy and friendly, but beware! Not all is as it seems. Though they appear to be cute and cuddly ants, they are actually wingless wasps, complete with a painful sting. Velvet ants are often seen quickly scuttling along the ground, as if in a great hurry. They may travel long distances in search of a bee or wasp nest, in which to lay their eggs. When the eggs hatch, the young eat the larvae in the nest.

Male velvet ants are equally colourful and just as hairy, but don't have a sting. Instead, they have wings and spend their time flying around in search of females.

Four-spotted velvet ant, North America. The four-spotted velvet ant gives off a particular smell to warn off predators.

Velvet ants squeak loudly when they are frightened.

Australian honeypot ant, Australia.
Replete honeypot ants have membranes
around their abdomen which stretch as
they fill up with nectar.

Australian honeypot ant

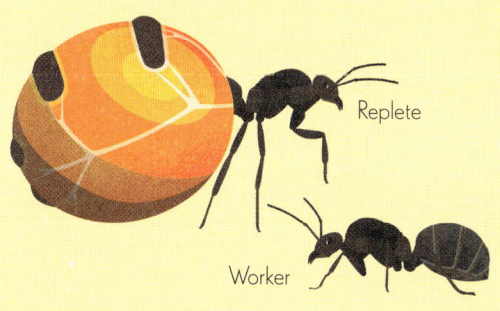

Replete

Worker

Where do you keep your honey? In a jar? In the cupboard? If you were a honeypot ant, you might store it in your stomach, so that the rest of your colony had something to eat when conditions were harsh! During the summer months, honeypot ants feed on nectar. But during the winter, there are very few flowers to forage from. In order to feed themselves, honeypot ants have an ingenious solution. Special workers, called repletes, guzzle down so much honey that their abdomen swells up to the size of a grape. Then they hang from the roof of the nest and act as "honey dispensers", regurgitating a sugary snack for any hungry ants that pass.

Rival ant colonies have been known to raid and steal the sugar-filled repletes of their neighbours!

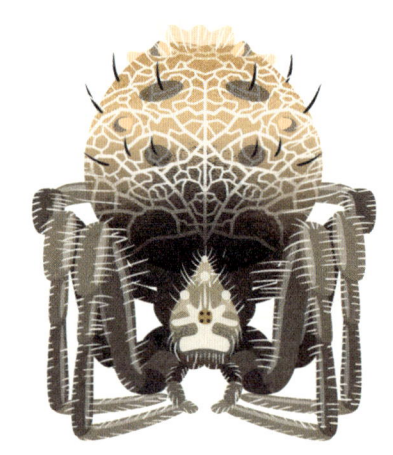

Bolas spider

What do you picture when you think of a spider web? Probably not a single thread, dangling down, ending in a tiny ball that glistens in the moonlight. But that is exactly what the bolas spider creates with its silk! The ball is called a bolas, and it is super sticky — perfect for capturing flying insects, such as moths.

After nightfall, the bolas spider emerges and waits. When a moth flutters within striking distance, the spider swings its sticky weapon through the air. If it manages to hit the moth, the spider then reels the strand back in. It either gobbles up its meal there and then, or wraps it up in silk and stores it as a snack for later.

Bolas spider, Australia.
The bolas spider's body is covered in tiny hairs that help it to sense when prey is near.

The bolas spider's sticky silk has the scent of female moths, which lures in males.

Common earwig

An old European superstition suggests that these small, nocturnal insects love nothing better than to crawl into people's ears while they sleep! Although this myth is totally untrue, the idea was so widespread it even gave the earwig its name. In reality, when earwigs come out of their hiding places at night, they seek out dead plant and animal matter to eat — not earwax. Their appetite for rotting food makes earwigs an important part of their ecosystem's clean-up crew as they recycle nutrients back into the soil.

Female earwigs are devoted mothers. Once a female has laid her eggs, she guards them and keeps them clean by licking them until they hatch. She also brings food to the young nymphs.

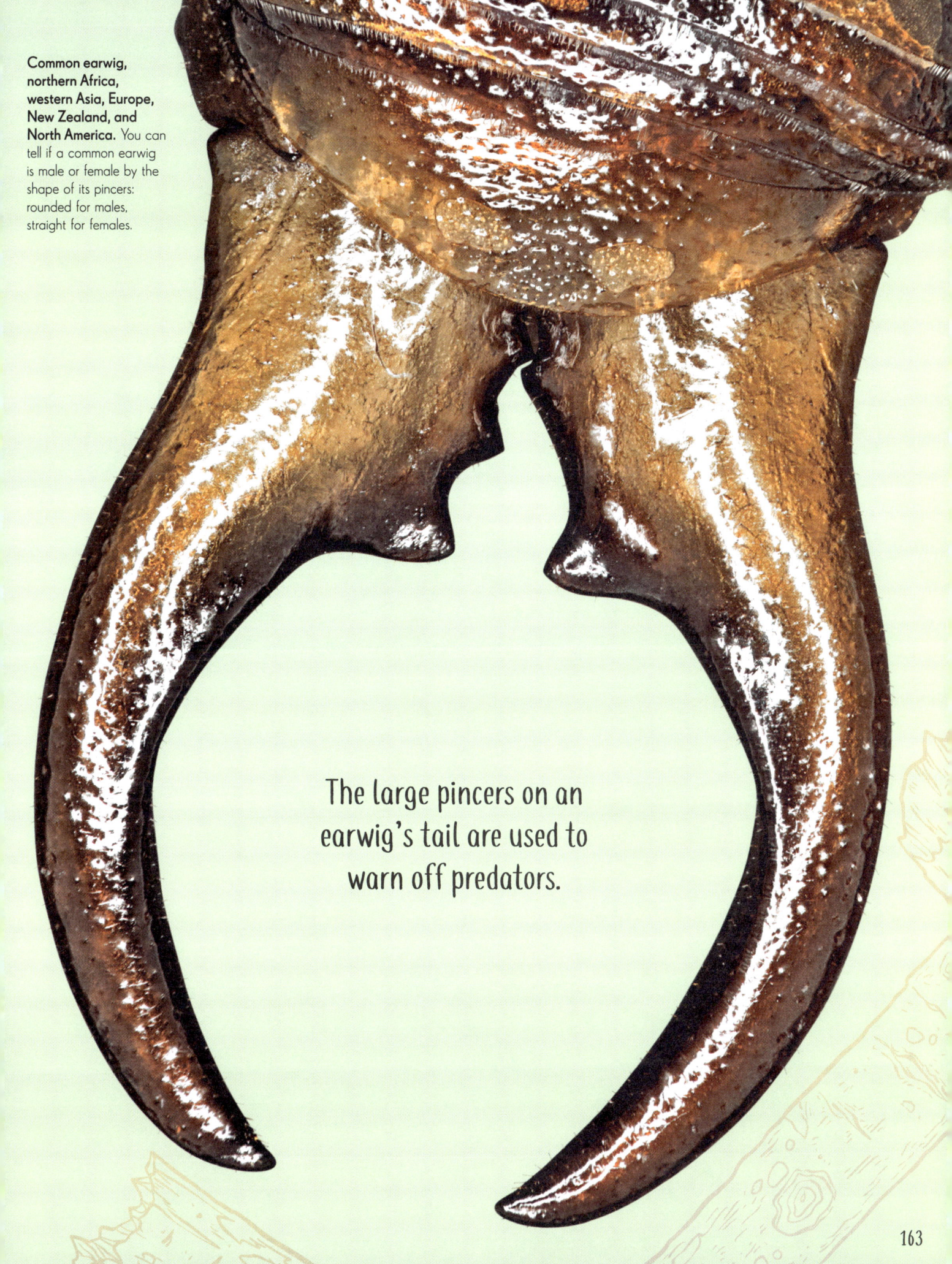

Common earwig, northern Africa, western Asia, Europe, New Zealand, and North America. You can tell if a common earwig is male or female by the shape of its pincers: rounded for males, straight for females.

The large pincers on an earwig's tail are used to warn off predators.

Pied hoverfly

Danger! Danger! It's a striped flying insect, it's going to hurt me! Or at least that's what hoverflies want you to think. In truth, hoverflies do not bite or sting, and have no interest in causing you pain. They are big pretenders that copy the colouring of bees and wasps to keep themselves safe.

Look close enough and you will see that hoverflies only have two wings, whilst bees and wasps have four. They also have much bigger, rounder eyes — and no sting. Hoverflies are like bees and wasps in one important way though, they are great pollinators and can often be spotted hovering around flowers in search of a tasty slurp of nectar.

Hoverflies fly with a distinctive darting movement and can fly forwards, backwards, and sideways.

Pied hoverfly, northern Africa, Asia, Europe, and North America.
The pied hoverfly's giant eyes cannot move, but are big enough to see in multiple directions at once.

Tsetse fly

Adult

Larva

If there's one thing tsetse flies are good at, it's eating. And as they feed on blood, that's bad news for the people where they live. Many tsetse flies carry tiny parasites in their saliva, which they can pass on to the people they bite, infecting them with a deadly disease called sleeping sickness.

Female tsetse flies need to eat blood so they can feed their babies. Most flies lay lots of eggs in one go, but tsetse flies do things differently. They produce just one egg at a time, which hatches inside their body. There, the larva feeds on a special kind of milk. The female only gives birth to her plump larva once it is ready to transform into an adult.

A tsetse fly can drink twice its own body weight in blood during a single meal.

Tsetse fly, central and western Africa. Female tsetse flies carry their larva for about 10 days before giving birth.

Seven-spot ladybird

The spiky bristles on the body of some ladybird larvae put off hungry birds.

Seven-spot ladybird, northern Africa, Asia, and Europe. Ladybird larvae shed their skin several times to grow bigger before they transform into adults.

Like all beetles, ladybirds start life as a larva, which looks nothing at all like the adult. Seven-spot ladybird larvae are sausage-shaped with orange spots and bristles! They stalk along branches and leaves in search of juicy aphids to eat. After around a month, a larva finds a hidden spot and becomes a pupa with a hard outer case. Inside, it is transforming into its adult form.

Childhood tales will have you believe that the number of spots on an adult ladybird's back tells you how old it is, but that's not true. The number of spots tells you which species the ladybird belongs to. They can have as many as 24 spots, but some ladybirds don't have any.

Male

Female

Red weaver ant-mimicking spider

High in the canopy of a humid jungle, a colony of weaver ants marches along a branch. At first glance, nothing appears out of the ordinary. But, look closer, and you will find that there is a trickster within their ranks… One of the ants is not an ant at all, but a red weaver ant-mimicking spider. The spider pretends to be an ant to keep it safe from predators. Red weaver ants can spray acid and give a nasty bite, so attackers avoid them. The female spider's disguise is almost perfect, and the male's isn't bad either. That is, until he opens his jaws. They are shaped like an ant's head, but when open they look like an ant divided in half!

The red weaver ant-mimicking spider
holds its front legs up above its head,
so they look like antennae.

Common horsefly, Asia and Europe. Horseflies have big, beautiful eyes. They see extremely well and the patterns may help with this.

Common horsefly

Only female horseflies bite, as they need the nutrient-rich blood in order to produce eggs.

Horseflies are experts at tracking down their prey. They are attracted to both the heat of animals' bodies and the carbon dioxide they release when they breathe. Using these signals, horseflies hone in on all kinds of large mammals, such as cows, horses, and even people. They are also silent fliers, so they can land without being detected on their hosts.

While some blood-sucking insects inject a numbing substance when they bite, horseflies do not. They also don't have needle-like mouthparts that slip neatly in and out of skin. Instead, they saw at skin until it starts to bleed, then soak up the blood with their sponge-like tongue. Ouch!

Two-coloured mason bee

**The picky two-coloured mason bee
will only lay eggs in the empty shells
of a few types of snail.**

Not all bees live in hives. They can make their homes in all kinds of places: underground, in plant stems, and even in cow dung. Two-coloured mason bees choose snail shells. Females are picky about the shells they select — they can't be too large, too small, too dark inside, or too light. Only the best for their babies!

Once a female has found her perfect shell, how does she turn it into a home for her larvae? After laying each egg inside, she adds a ball of pollen beside it for the larva to snack on. When the shell is full, she seals it with chewed leaves and shell fragments. Finally, she covers the shell with grass and fallen leaves to disguise it.

Two-coloured mason bee, northern Africa, Asia, and Europe. Male bees of this species are not as brightly coloured as the females.

Castor bean tick

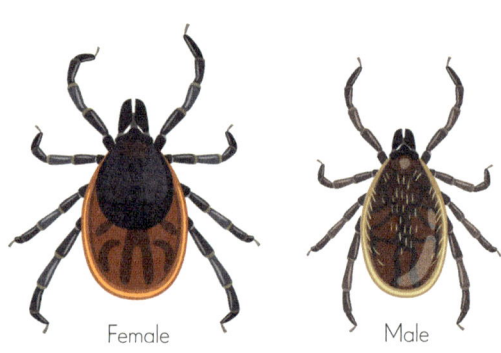

Female

Male

Ticks are parasites. They must feed on the blood of other animals in order to grow. Castor bean ticks are often found in grass and woodland areas, where they wait on the tips of leaves so they can grab onto passing victims. Once a tick has bitten an animal, it remains attached and can feed for hours or even days before dropping off.

Before eating, castor bean ticks are small and hard to notice. If you looked very closely, you might spot a little, eight-legged creature that looked a bit like a spider. After a good meal of blood, it's a different story! A tick will keep sucking until it fills up, and can swell to the size of a pea.

Ticks can spread diseases as they transfer germs when they bite.

Castor bean tick, northern Africa, western Asia, and Europe.
Backward-pointing barbs keep the tick's mouthparts buried in its host's skin.

Sawfly larvae are often found feeding in large groups.

Spotted regal sawfly

These plump green creatures look a lot like caterpillars, don't they? But unlike caterpillars, they won't turn into butterflies or moths. They will become sawflies, which are close relatives of ants, bees, and wasps. You can tell sawfly larvae apart by their number of prolegs — that's the little leg-like blobs dotted along the bottom of their bodies. Caterpillars have a maximum of five pairs, but sawflies have six or more.

Just like caterpillars, sawfly larvae are leaf eaters. They usually eat from the edge of the leaf down towards the centre, and they can rapidly strip trees bare. Spotted regal sawfly larvae love the taste of many different types of leaves, including birch, maple, and ash.

Spotted regal sawfly, Europe. Sawfly larvae curl their bodies into an "S" or "C" shape when they feel threatened.

A close relative of the black widow from the USA,
the redback is small, but has a big reputation!

Redback spider, Australia. Female
redbacks are black with red-orange
markings on their back. Males are smaller
and brown with white and red markings.

Redback spider

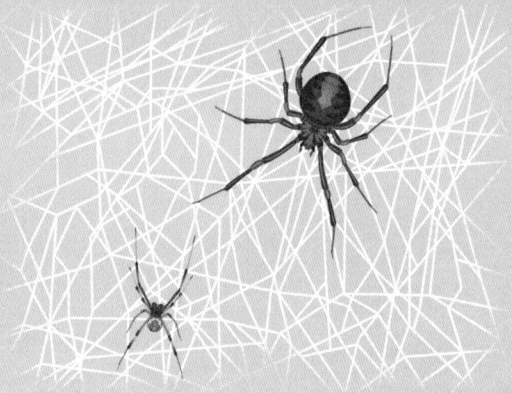

Redback spiders are found across Australia and often live close to people. Females make webs that are a messy tangle of threads in sheltered spots, such as log piles and sheds. They sit and wait for insects to be ensnared by sticky lines that extend to the ground. Males are much smaller than females and do not make webs. Instead, they wander around, sometimes lurking on the edge of webs belonging to females and hoping not to be eaten!

The bright markings on a redback's abdomen mean danger! They are venomous spiders, and the female's bite is particularly dangerous to humans. But redbacks don't usually leave their webs, so bites are rare.

Malaysian stalk-eyed fly

How do you tell how strong someone is? By the size of their muscles? By the number of weights they can lift? Well, if you were a stalk-eyed fly, it would be by the distance between their eyes. Stalk-eyes flies have long eyestalks, but they don't help these insects to see. They are used to impress potential mates. Males go head-to-head, measuring their eyestalks against each other. The widest eyestalks win. However, these odd-looking features can make life more tricky. Seeing, flying, and escaping predators are all easier without your eyes on long, delicate stalks.

Male

Male

Female

Female stalk-eyed flies have shorter eyestalks than males.

Malaysian stalk-eyed fly, southern Asia and Southeast Asia. The eyespan of some stalk-eyed flies is longer than the length of their body.

Acorn weevil

All weevils have long, thin snouts, but even by weevil standards, the snout of the acorn weevil is impressive!

Acorn weevil, Europe.
Hairy footpads help this weevil to grip onto many surfaces.

The summer sun is blazing, and green acorns are growing, firmly attached to the tree. Attracted to these ripening nuts are female acorn weevils, searching for somewhere to lay their eggs. Using the sensitive antennae on her extra-long snout, a female finds the perfect acorn, then starts to drill her way through the shell using the small but sharp jaws at the end of her snout. She then lays an egg inside the nut, before plugging the hole with her own poo! After a couple of weeks, the weevil larva hatches and eats the inside of the acorn. Eventually, as the seasons change, the acorn falls to the ground and the larva escapes, before digging into the ground to wait to transform into an adult.

Yellow fever mosquito

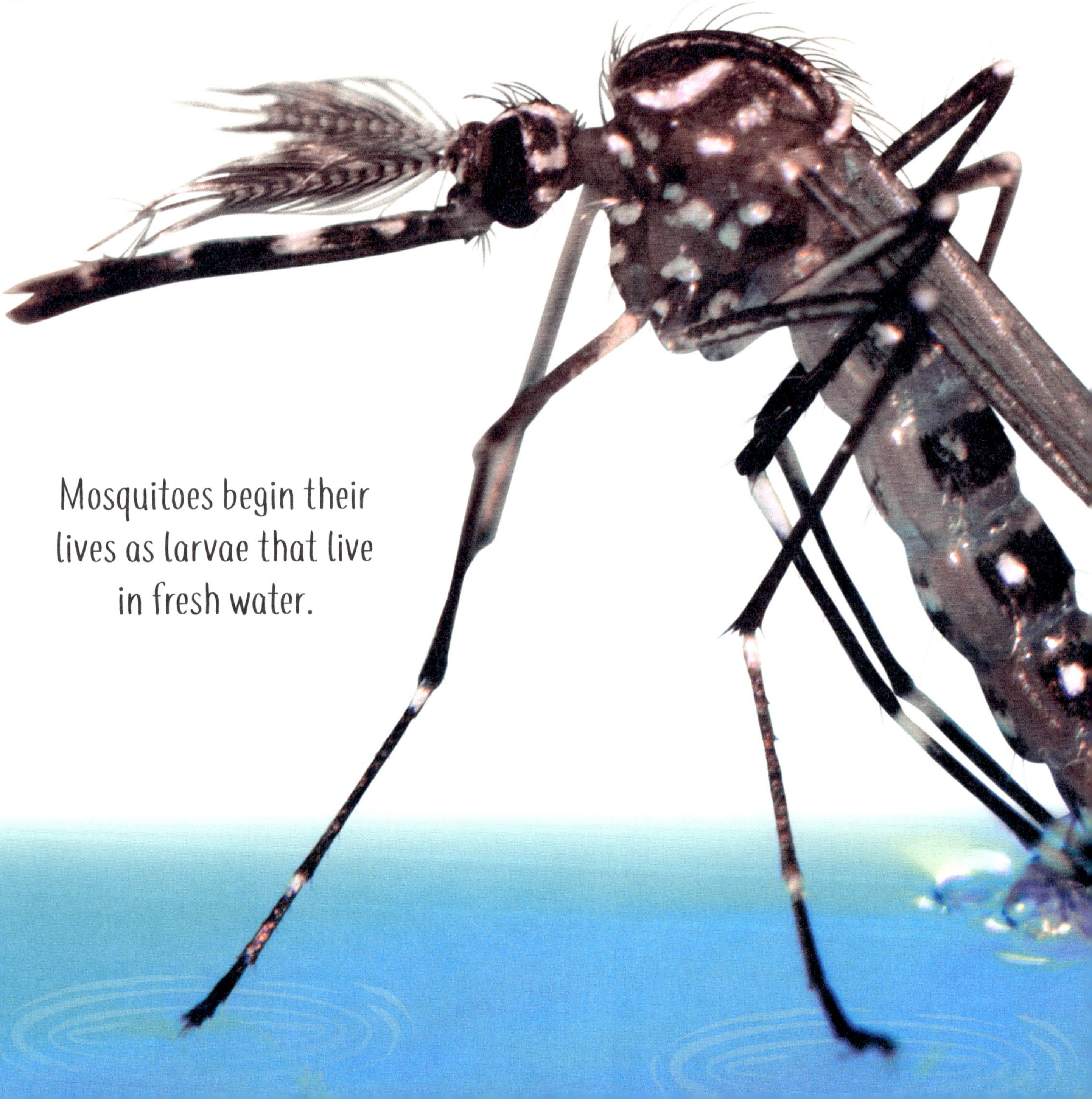

Mosquitoes begin their lives as larvae that live in fresh water.

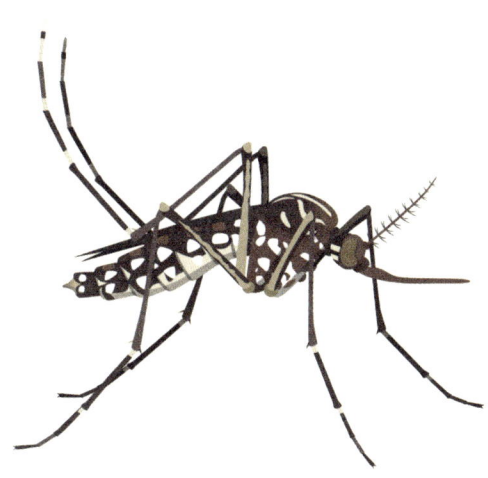

Zzzzzzz... Just the sound of a mosquito in flight can make you feel itchy, can't it? These pesky flies are famous for sucking the blood of animals and spreading deadly diseases, such as yellow fever. When a mosquito bites, it injects saliva into the wound — this is what makes you itch — and it's also how parasites and viruses are moved from person to person. However, not all mosquitoes bite. Only female mosquitoes have the needle-like mouthparts capable of piercing through skin. Male mosquitos are smaller than females and have mouthparts that are better suited to drinking nectar from flowers. This is because it is only females that need to eat blood as it helps them produce healthy eggs, which they lay in water.

Yellow fever mosquito, Africa. This male yellow fever mosquito is emerging from its pupa into the air.

Harlequin ladybird

The pupae of ladybirds are often found stuck to the undersides of leaves. They may be similar in colour to the adult ladybirds that will emerge. The larva's old, moulted, spiky exoskeleton can be seen at the base of the pupa.

Tiger mosquito

Tiger mosquito larvae make a comma-shaped pupa that hangs under the surface of still water. When they are disturbed, they tumble through the water, giving them the nickname "tumblers".

False burnet moth

False burnet moths become pupae inside mesh-like cocoons, which they hang from a leaf by a strand of silk. The open cocoon is thought to provide protection from predators, while also letting rain drain through.

An opening at the bottom of the cocoon lets the pupa get rid of its old moulted exoskeleton.

Bluebottle fly

The pupae of bluebottles are surrounded by an extra layer of protection — the hardened exoskeleton of the larva, which is also known as a puparium. The emerging adult inflates a sac on its head to break out of the puparium.

Cloudless sulphur butterfly

The pupa of a butterfly is called a chrysalis. The chrysalis of the cloudless sulphur butterfly is cleverly disguised to look like a folded leaf and can be green, yellow, or pink.

Domestic silk moth

Domestic silk moth caterpillars, also known as silkworms, create an extra case around themselves, called a cocoon, while they are a pupa. The cocoon is spun from threads of silk that can be used to make fabric.

Pupae

Some insects completely change their body shape partway through their life — just think of a caterpillar and a butterfly. While it is changing, an insect becomes a pupa, which often has a special hard case. Inside the pupa, the body parts of the larva are rearranged until they form the shape of the adult insect. The cases of pupae are often very tough, to protect the insect from danger whilst it cannot defend itself, and they can be camouflaged, too. When a larva becomes a pupa, it is called pupation, and when an adult breaks out of its pupa, it is called emergence.

European rhinoceros beetle

The pupae of beetles often look a lot like the adults. Rhinoceros beetle pupae already have their distinctive horn on their head. These pupae are usually hidden safely underground.

Orange-spotted tiger clearwing

The chrysalis of the orange-spotted tiger clearwing has a remarkable method of camouflage — it acts like a mirror! The surrounding plants are reflected in its polished surface, which confuses predators and keeps it safe.

Golden tortoise beetle

Golden tortoise beetle larvae cover themselves in their own poo to put off predators!

The shimmering surface on the wing cases of the golden tortoise beetle is as bright and shiny as a brand new coin. With four "legs", it also makes the beetle look a bit like a tortoise! And that's not where the tortoise similarities end. When golden tortoise beetles are frightened, they can pull their legs, head, and antennae under their domed shell to protect them from harm. Unlike a tortoise, though, these beetles have a special trick. When they feel threatened, they can change colour from glimmering gold to vibrant red. This puts off predators, so the beetles can carry on doing what they like best — nibbling on leaves, especially those of sweet potatoes.

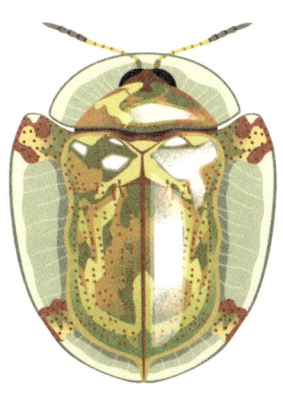

Golden tortoise beetle, North and South America. The glittering shell of this beetle divides in two to reveal its wings when it flies.

Meadow froghopper, northern Africa, Asia, and Europe. Young froghoppers hide themselves in a foamy home and only leave once they are fully grown.

Meadow froghopper

Some people call froghoppers "spittlebugs" and the froth they produce is also known as "cuckoo spit"!

Sometimes, in the spring, mysterious foamy blobs appear on the leaves and stems of plants. They look a little like someone had a bubble bath and let the bubbles overflow! But this frothy liquid isn't made of soap suds, it's made of plant sap. The tiny nymph of an insect called a froghopper guzzles the plant's juices, then pumps them out of its bottom, along with lots of little gas bubbles, to make itself a thick protective coat.

When it is fully grown, the froghopper has another remarkable method of escaping danger — it can leap more than 100 times its own length. That's like you jumping over a football field in just one leap.

Sea skater

Sea skaters are the only insects
to live on the ocean.

Imagine being able to walk on water! That's exactly what these
incredible insects can do. To keep themselves afloat, sea skaters
use their long legs to spread a special wax all over their body, which
repels water. They are also covered in tiny hairs, which trap a layer of
air around them, helping them to survive brief spells underwater and
pop back up to the surface.

Sea skaters spend their entire life on the surface of the ocean, either
near the coast or permanently out at sea. There is little shade from
the hot sun here and few places to hide, so sea skaters make an
easy snack for passing predators. However, they can leap high into
the air to escape predators — or large waves.

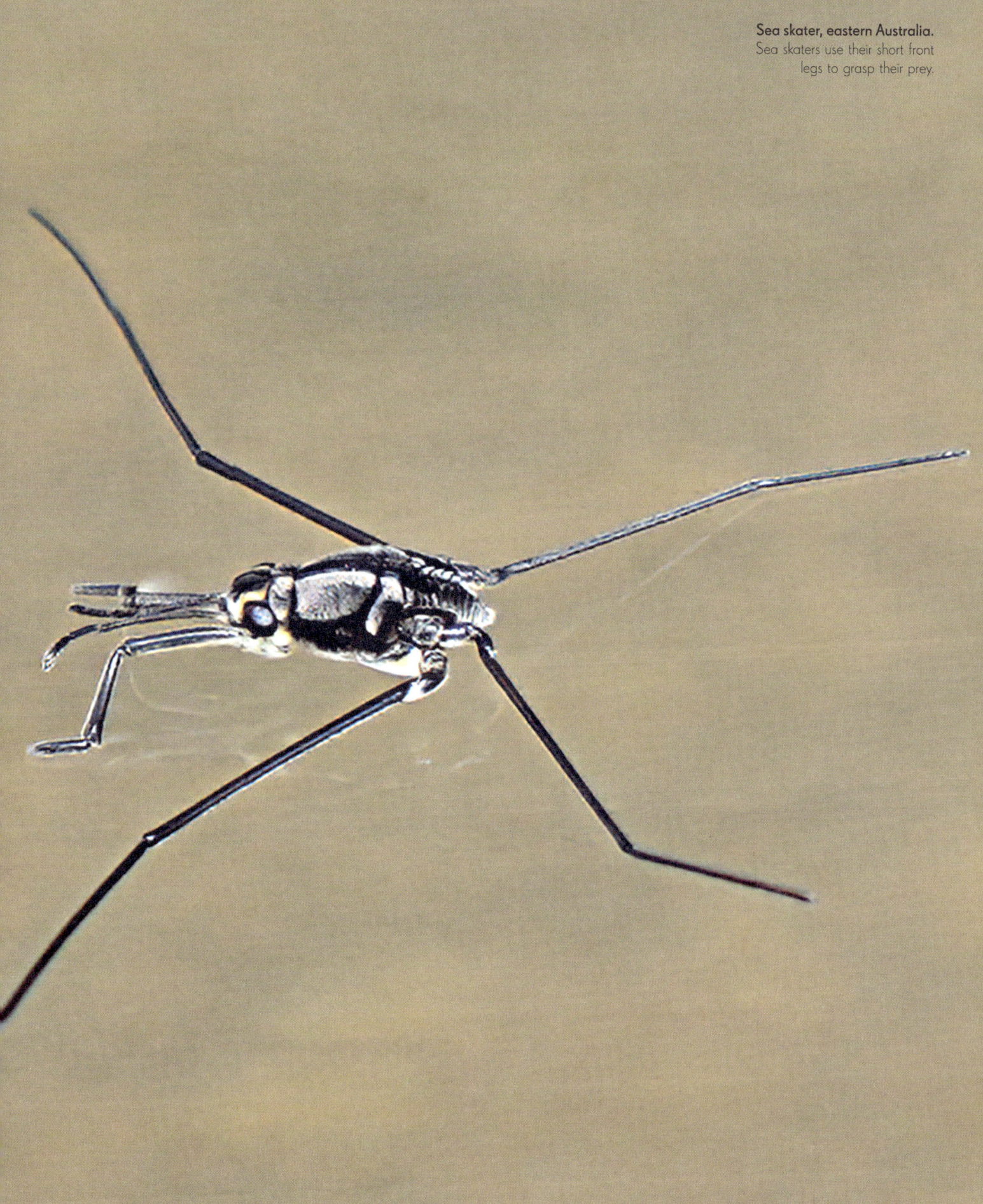

Sea skater, eastern Australia.
Sea skaters use their short front
legs to grasp their prey.

Young planthoppers can launch themselves
into the air at about 3 m (10 ft) per second.

Bristle-tailed planthopper

B oing! When frightened, planthoppers catapult themselves into the air, making a bold and speedy escape. Often, these powerful leaps send the tiny acrobats tumbling, somersaulting many times on their way to safety. When they come to land on a new plant, planthoppers immediately get to work feeding again. Leaping is hungry work! Luckily, these bugs specialize in eating the energy-rich, sugary sap found within the leaves and stems of plants. After digesting the sap, young planthoppers, called nymphs, make any excess sugar into wax, which can form a funny-looking tail. Scientists think these tails may help the nymphs stay stable in the air and prevent them from spinning out of control.

Bristle-tailed planthopper, eastern North America. The waxy tail of this planthopper nymph looks like a bundle of sticks.

Cochineal

In the 17th century, the dye made from cochineal bugs was one of Mexico's most valuable exports — second only to silver.

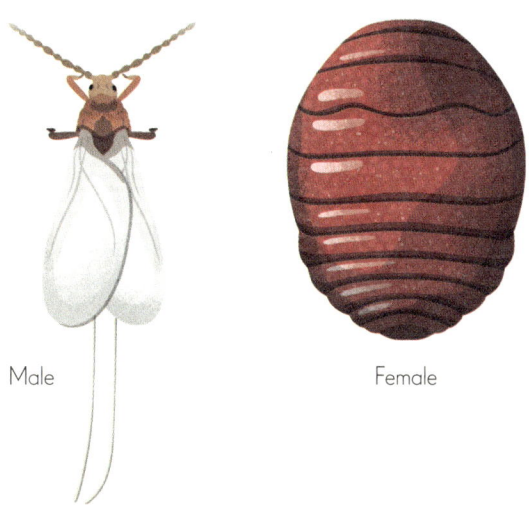

Male

Female

In the hot deserts of Mexico, prickly pear cactus leaves are often covered in patches of white fluff. Is it a disease? Lichen? Mould? No! It's the cotton-like, waxy covering of cochineal insects. Snuggled between the spines, female cochineal insects can spend almost their whole lives attached to the thick leaves of a cactus, slurping out its juices. The white fluff protects them from predators and the scorching sun. There they wait for a male to fly by, so they can mate.

To further protect them from predators, cochineal bugs have bodies bursting with a special acid. This chemical is a vibrant red and humans have used it for centuries as a dye, to stain everything from paint and fabric to makeup and even food.

Cochineal, southern North America and northern South America. Both nymphs and adult female cochineal insects produce a white fluff that stops them losing water in the heat.

Slender springtail

Slender springtail, Europe.
The hairs covering the bodies of springtails repel water so they do not drown.

Tiny to us, but giant to other springtails, slender springtails can reach 5 mm (0.2 in) in length — that's just less than the width of a pencil. These springtails come in many colours, including brown, grey, black, yellow, and orange, with bold patterns and stripes. They can be found in damp places, such as piles of rotting leaves.

When frightened, some springtails can jump more than 60 times their own height to escape from danger. They get their name from their fork-shaped tail, known as a furcula (fer-kyoo-la), which they hold under their abdomen. To make their impressive jumps, they release the furcula, which swings down and catapults the springtails high into the air, sending them spinning backwards to safety.

A springtail can spin backwards
368 times in one second!

A female aphid can give birth to a baby aphid that is already pregnant with a daughter of her own!

Pea aphid

Tiny green specks stuck to a stem, a sprinkle of pale dots on the underside of a leaf… If they didn't affect the growth of food crops, it might be easy for aphids to go unnoticed. However, these little green bugs have a terrible reputation among farmers and gardeners. When they move from plant to plant, they use their pointed mouthparts to suck up tasty plant juices, which can spread many different plant diseases. They can also damage leaves and fruit as they slurp up sap. Luckily, aphids are an attractive snack to larger insects, such as ladybirds, lacewings, and crab spiders, which help keep their numbers from growing too high.

Pea aphid, northern Africa, Asia, and Europe. This female pea aphid is giving birth to a baby that is a clone of her, meaning the baby is exactly the same as its mother.

House pseudoscorpion

Our homes are full of tiny insects, such as clothes moths, booklice, and dust mites that munch on our things. But did you know that many places are also patrolled by little predators that keep these pests in check? House pseudoscorpions are arachnids and look a lot like their cousins, the scorpions, but without the tail and in miniature — they are less than 5 mm (0.2 in) long. These helpful creatures find their way into our homes in a rather remarkable way — they hitchhike! When they want to move to a new place, they simply grab onto a passing insect, such as a bee, beetle, or wasp, and get a lift.

Pseudoscorpions have been around for roughly 390 million years.

House pseudoscorpion, Africa, Australia, Europe, and North America. House pseudoscorpions use their pincers to grab onto a passing insect.

**Banana lacewing bug, southern
Asia and Southeast Asia.**
When light bounces off the
banana lacewing bug's wings,
they sparkle like stained glass.

Banana lacewing bug

T he beautiful banana lacewing bug is not always a welcome visitor. It lives in large colonies on the underside of leaves, but the plants it chooses are often those that humans like to grow as crops. Both adult banana lacewing bugs and their nymphs use needle-like mouthparts to suck sap from the leaves of banana, coconut, turmeric, ginger, and cardamom plants. Their meals leave behind ugly spots, which makes the crops more difficult to sell, and they can spread plant diseases.

Lacewing bugs get their name from the delicate lacy pattern of veins on their wings. The membrane inbetween these veins can make colourful patterns when light reflects off it.

Lacewing bugs are tiny — they are smaller than a grain of rice.

Despite their name, cat fleas can be
found on cats, dogs, and even people!

Cat flea

Have you ever seen a cat scratching furiously at its coat, desperate to relieve an unbearable itch? It probably had fleas! These tiny parasites hop through the fur and feathers of animals, feeding on their blood. The adults feed by piercing a host's skin with sharp, pointy mouthparts then sucking up their blood through a tube.

Flea larvae have a different approach. They don't live on a host, so can't feed directly on its blood. Instead, they mainly gobble up the poo of the adults, also known as flea dirt, which has fallen to the ground. Once they have transformed into adults, they use their long back legs to leap onto an animal. Fleas can jump more than 100 times the length of their body!

Cat flea, worldwide, except the Arctic and Antarctic. There are thousands of different flea species. Cat fleas are the most common and are found all over the world.

Varroa mite

Insects may be small, but even they get parasites. Mites are tiny cousins of spiders and many live on other animals. Sneaky varroa mites hitch a ride on the backs of honeybees and suck their haemolymph (insect blood) as a snack. Sometimes, several mites can be found travelling on a single bee. Once the bee reaches its nest, the mites hop off and make their way to the hive nursery, where the honeybees keep their eggs safe. Inside the nursery, female varroa mites lay their own eggs. When the young mites hatch, they feed on the bee larvae as they develop. This can makes the bees weak and even kill them. A large infestation of mites can destroy a whole hive.

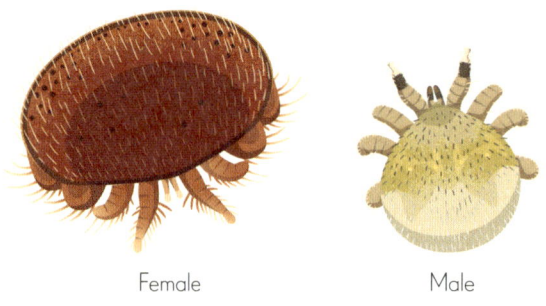

Female

Male

Varroa mites are deadly to honeybees — they can wipe out a whole colony in a year.

Varroa mite, Africa, Asia, Europe, and North America.
The little varroa mite has a round body and eight short legs, which it uses to cling to a bee's body.

Tree of life

We use the word "bug" to describe many different animals. Usually, "bug" refers to an invertebrate, or animal without a backbone, that lives on land. However, bugs can be split up into many smaller groups, such as "arthropods", which are bugs with a hard exoskeleton and a segmented body. Scientists, however, use the word bug for just one of these small groups — the "true bugs", which includes shield bugs and aphids. The tree of life shows how closely these groups are related to each other.

Termites

Mantises

Grasshoppers

Cockroaches

Stick insects

Earwigs

Leaf insects

Pseudoscorpions

Silverfish

Scorpions

Sun spiders

Springtails

Harvestmen

Whip spiders

Ticks

Mites

Spiders

Vinegaroons

Arachnids

Arachnids are arthropods with a hard exoskeleton, a body made of two sections, and eight jointed legs. Unlike insects, they don't have antennae or wings. Most are predators and some are highly venomous. This group includes spiders, scorpions, ticks, and mites.

Worms

Worms have a soft body made up of many segments. They have no exoskeleton or legs, but can be excellent at swimming and burrowing. They may be found in sand, soil or water — anywhere they are not at risk of drying out.

Worms

Molluscs

Most molluscs live in the ocean, and some can be enormous, but those that live on land are generally smaller than a guinea pig. This group of animals usually has a soft body, but some, such as snails, have a shell to help protect them.

Slugs and snails

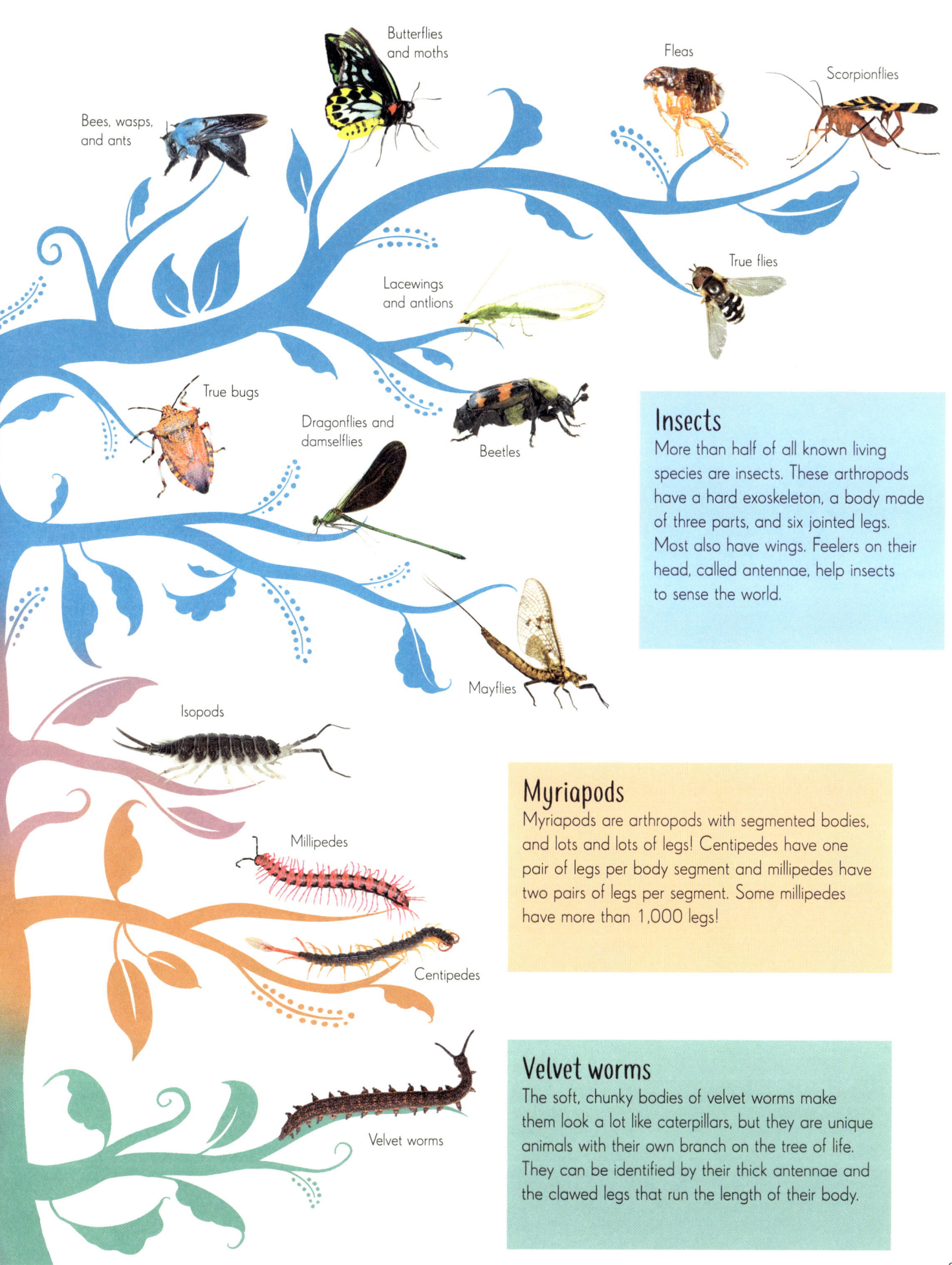

Butterflies and moths

Fleas

Scorpionflies

Bees, wasps, and ants

True flies

Lacewings and antlions

True bugs

Dragonflies and damselflies

Beetles

Insects
More than half of all known living species are insects. These arthropods have a hard exoskeleton, a body made of three parts, and six jointed legs. Most also have wings. Feelers on their head, called antennae, help insects to sense the world.

Mayflies

Isopods

Myriapods
Myriapods are arthropods with segmented bodies, and lots and lots of legs! Centipedes have one pair of legs per body segment and millipedes have two pairs of legs per segment. Some millipedes have more than 1,000 legs!

Millipedes

Centipedes

Velvet worms
The soft, chunky bodies of velvet worms make them look a lot like caterpillars, but they are unique animals with their own branch on the tree of life. They can be identified by their thick antennae and the clawed legs that run the length of their body.

Velvet worms

Glossary

abdomen Rear section of the body of an insect or arachnid. The abdomen is usually the largest section and contains many important organs

adaptation Feature of an animal that helps it to survive in its habitat. For example, the long front legs of a whip spider help it to sense its way in the dark

allergy Reaction to a substance, such as pollen, that causes a person to experience symptoms including itching, swelling, redness, and difficulty breathing

antennae Sensitive feelers on the head of an arthropod, usually found in pairs. Arthropods use their antennae to feel, smell, and taste the world around them

aposematism When an animal has bright colours to warn other animals that it is venomous or poisonous. Common aposematic colours are red, orange, and yellow or yellow-and-black stripes. Some animals have bright colours to pretend they are toxic as a defence

aquatic Description of an animal that lives underwater

arachnid Type of arthropod that has eight legs and two body sections. Spiders, sun spiders, scorpions, and mites are all types of arachnid

arthropod Type of invertebrate with a hard exoskeleton that is divided into sections. Insects and arachnids are types of arthropod

brood Young of an animal that have hatched or been born at the same time

camouflage Colour or pattern that disguises an animal where it lives, to help it hide from predators or prey

carbon dioxide Invisible waste gas that animals breathe out

carrion Dead body of an animal

chrysalis Pupa of a butterfly. Many chrysalises are camouflaged and look like leaves

clone Individual animal that is identical to another individual animal. For example, baby aphids are identical to their mother

cocoon Case made by an animal to surround its pupa to camouflage and protect it. Cocoons are often made of silk

colony Large group of related animals that live and work together to help the colony survive. Some ants, bees, wasps, and termites live in colonies with a queen that lays eggs and workers that collect food and defend their home

egg Capsule that hatches into a baby animal. The eggs of slugs and snails have a soft shell, while the eggs of insects have a hard shell

emergence When an adult insect breaks out of its pupa

exoskeleton Hard outer covering of arthropods. Exoskeletons are divided into sections to allow arthropods to move

fang Sharp mouthpart that delivers venom

host Animal that a parasite relies on for food

insect Type of arthropod with three pairs of legs and a body divided into three sections. These are the head, thorax (in the middle), and the abdomen (at the back). Butterflies, moths, beetles, dragonflies, cockroaches, true bugs, flies, ants, bees, and wasps are all types of insect

invertebrate Animal with no backbone including insects, spiders, and snails

larva Young of some insects that often resemble grubs, and look very different to their adult form. Larvae transform into adults by complete metamorphosis. Caterpillars are a type of larva

metamorphosis When an animal has a dramatic change in its shape as it grows older. Some animals undergo complete metamorphosis and completely change shape. For example, when a caterpillar changes into a butterfly. Others undergo incomplete metamorphosis, and only change shape a little

moult When an arthropod sheds its old exoskeleton in order to grow bigger or to go through metamorphosis. Animals can look quite different after they have moulted

mouthparts Biting or chewing appendages around an arthropod's mouth that they use to eat with

mucus Slimy gel made by some animals. Slugs and snails produce mucus to help them glide over the ground

nectar Sweet, sugary liquid made by flowers. Insects and birds visit flowers to drink nectar

nocturnal Description of an animal that is active at night

nutrients Essential types of food that animals need to live and grow

nymph Young of some insects that look similar to their adult form. Nymphs transform into adults by incomplete metamorphosis. For example, true bugs and grasshoppers are nymphs when young

ovipositor Organ found at the rear of the abdomen of female insects used to lay their eggs

oxygen Invisible gas that animals need to breathe. It is released by algae and plants, and is one of the main gases in air

parasite Animal that lives on another host animal, or inside its body, and causes the host harm. Parasites feed on the host animal and cannot live without it. For example, fleas and ticks are parasites that feed on the blood of other animals

poison Harmful substance made by an animal as a defence. Poison often stays in the skin, and an attacker is poisoned if it touches or eats the poisonous animal

pollen Dust-like grains made by flowers. Pollen spreads on the wind or with the help of animals called pollinators. When pollen is moved from flower to flower, it allows the flowers to produce seeds. Some arthropods eat pollen

pollinator Animal that moves pollen between plants

predator Animal that hunts another animal, called prey, for food

prey Animal that is hunted by a predator

proboscis Long, straw-like mouthparts of butterflies and moths that they usually use to drink nectar from flowers

pupa Name for an insect that is undergoing metamorphosis. Insects emerge from their pupa in their adult form

sap Sugary liquid produced by plants. It moves around inside the trunk and branches, a bit like blood in animals

shell Tough covering that an animal makes to protect parts of its body

silk Thin, tough fibre produced by spiders and some larvae. Many spiders use sticky silk to catch prey, while some larvae use it to create a cocoon to protect themselves when they are a pupa

species Particular type of animal, plant, or other living thing. For example, glasswings and Queen Alexandra's birdwings are different species of butterfly. Members of the same species can breed together to produce young, but they usually cannot breed with other species

spiracle Hole found in the side of insects through which they breathe

stinger Sharp, needle-like organ used by animals to deliver venom. Stingers are often found at the rear of an animal

tentacle Soft, long body part used by animals to sense their environment

toxic Harmful

vein Fluid-filled tube, often joined up in a network, that gives support to an insect's wings

venom Harmful liquid made by an animal. Venom is different from poison because it is delivered by stingers or a bite into prey or an attacker's body

web Network of sticky silk fibres made by a spider to capture prey

Visual guide

Fried egg earthworm, page 4
Archipheretima middletoni
Group: Worms
Length: 40 cm (16 in)
Location: Philippines

Johnston's whip spider, page 6
Damon johnstonii
Group: Whip spiders
Legspan: 32.5 cm (13 in)
Location: Central and western Africa

Queen Alexandra's birdwing, page 8
Ornithoptera alexandrae
Group: Butterflies and moths
Wingspan: 30 cm (12 in)
Location: Papua New Guinea

Atlas moth, page 10
Attacus atlas
Group: Butterflies and moths
Wingspan: 27 cm (11 in)
Location: Asia

Leopard slug, page 12
Limax maximus
Group: Slugs and snails
Length: 20 cm (8 in)
Location: Northern Africa and Europe

Giant West African snail, page 14
Archachatina marginata
Group: Slugs and snails
Length: 20 cm (8 in)
Location: Western Africa

Mediterranean medicinal leech, page 16
Hirudo verbana
Group: Worms
Length: 20 cm (8 in)
Location: Western Asia and Europe

Pink underwing moth, page 18
Phyllodes imperialis
Group: Butterflies and moths
Wingspan: 17 cm (7 in)
Location: Oceania

Hickory horned devil, page 22
Citheronia regalis
Group: Butterflies and moths
Wingspan: 15.5 cm (6 in)
Location: Eastern North America

Grant's sun spider, page 24
Galeodes granti
Group: Sun spiders
Length: 15 cm (6 in)
Location: Northeastern Africa and southwestern Asia

Giant vinegaroon, page 26
Mastigoproctus tohono
Group: Vinegaroons
Length: 15 cm (6 in)
Location: Southern North America

Mexican redknee tarantula, page 28
Brachypelma hamorii
Group: Spiders
Legspan: 15 cm (6 in)
Location: Mexico

Flagtail centipede, page 30
Alipes grandidieri
Group: Centipedes
Length: 15 cm (6 in)
Location: Eastern Africa

Oleander hawk moth, page 32
Daphnis nerii
Group: Butterflies and moths
Wingspan: 13 cm (5 in)
Location: Africa, Asia, and southern Europe

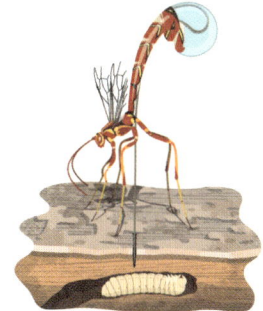

Long-tailed giant ichneumon wasp, page 34
Megarhyssa macrurus
Group: Ants, bees, and wasps
Length: 13 cm (5 in)
Location: Eastern North America

Devil's flower mantis, page 36
Idolomantis diabolica
Group: Praying mantises
Length: 13 cm (5 in)
Location: Eastern Africa

Brown forest harvestman, page 40
Eupoecilaema magnum
Group: Harvestmen
Legspan: 12 cm (5 in)
Location: Costa Rica

Deathstalker, page 42
Leiurus quinquestriatus
Group: Scorpions
Length: 11 cm (4 in)
Location: Northern Africa and southwestern Asia

Hissing cockroach, page 44
Gromphadorhina portentosa
Group: Cockroaches
Length: 10.2 cm (4 in)
Location: Madagascar

Indonesian leaf insect, page 46
Phyllium letiranti
Group: Stick insects
Length: 9.5 cm (4 in)
Location: Indonesia

Peanut bug, page 50
Fulgora laternaria
Group: True bugs
Length: 9 cm (4 in)
Location: Southern North America and northern South America

Black fat-tailed scorpion, page 52
Androctonus bicolor
Group: Scorpions
Length: 8 cm (3 in)
Location: Northern Africa and southwestern Asia

Green metalwing, page 54
Neurobasis chinensis
Group: Dragonflies
Wingspan: 8 cm (3 in)
Location: Eastern Asia and Southeast Asia

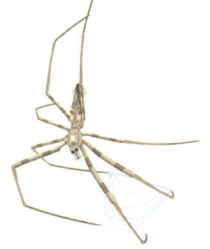

Ogre-faced spider, page 56
Asianopsis aspectans
Group: Spiders
Legspan: 7 cm (3 in)
Location: Cameroon

Phantom flutterer, page 58
Rhyothemis semihyalina
Group: Dragonflies
Wingspan: 7 cm (3 in)
Location: Africa and southwestern Asia

Orchid mantis, page 60
Hymenopus coronatus
Group: Praying mantises
Length: 7 cm (3 in)
Location: Southeast Asia

European mole cricket, page 62
Gryllotalpa gryllotalpa
Group: Grasshoppers
Length: 7 cm (3 in)
Location: Northern Africa, western Asia, and Europe

Green skipper, page 64
Telegonus habana
Group: Butterflies and moths
Wingspan: 7 cm (3 in)
Location: Northern Caribbean

Glasswing butterfly, page 66
Greta oto
Group: Butterflies and moths
Wingspan: 6.1 cm (2 in)
Location: Southern North America and northern South America

Soil termite, page 68
Macrotermes gilvus
Group: Cockroaches
Length: 6 cm (2 in) queen, 1.1 cm (0.4 in) worker
Location: Southeast Asia

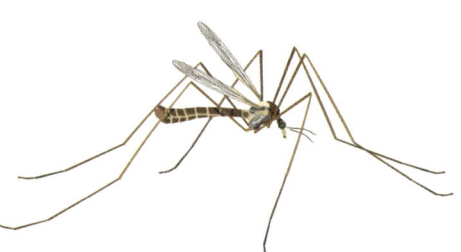

Marsh crane fly, page 70
Tipula oleracea
Group: Flies
Legspan: 6 cm (2 in)
Location: Northern Africa and Europe

Eciton army ant, page 72
Eciton burchellii
Group: Ants, bees, and wasps
Length: 6 cm queen (2 in); 3–12 mm (0.2–0.5 in) worker
Location: Southern North America and northern South America

Lichen katydid, page 74
Markia hystrix
Group: Grasshoppers
Length: 5.8 cm (2 in)
Location: Central America and northern South America

Black beauty stick insect, page 76
Peruphasma schultei
Group: Stick insects
Length: 5.5 cm (2 in)
Location: Peru

New Zealand velvet worm, page 78
Peripatoides novaezealandiae
Group: Velvet worms
Length: 5 cm (2 in)
Location: New Zealand

Picasso moth, page 80
Baorisa hieroglyphica
Group: Butterflies and moths
Wingspan: 5 cm (2 in)
Location: Southern Asia and Southeast Asia

Trilobite beetle, page 82
Platerodrilus paradoxus
Group: Beetles
Length: 5 cm (2 in)
Location: Southeast Asia

Saddleback caterpillar, page 84
Acharia stimuli
Group: Butterflies and moths
Wingspan: 4.3 cm (2 in)
Location: North America

Australian horror moth, page 86
Creatonotos gangis
Group: Butterflies and moths
Wingspan: 4 cm (2 in)
Location: Australia and
Southeast Asia

Asian dune cricket, page 88
Schizodactylus monstrosus
Group: Grasshoppers
Length: 4 cm (2 in)
Location: Southern Asia

Pharaoh cicada, page 90
Magicicada septendecim
Group: True bugs
Length: 4 cm (2 in)
Location: North America

Wheel bug, page 92
Arilus carinatus
Group: True bugs
Length: 3.8 cm (1 in)
Location: South America

Southern flannel moth, page 94
Megalopyge opercularis
Group: Butterflies and moths
Wingspan: 3.6 cm (1 in)
Location: Eastern North America

European hornet, page 96
Vespa crabro
Group: Ants, bees, and wasps
Length: 3.5 cm (1 in) queen,
2.5 cm (1 in) worker
Location: Asia and Europe

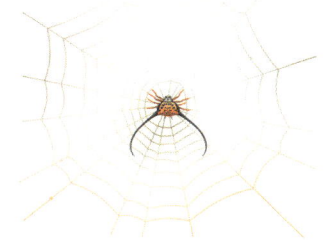

Long-horned orb weaver, page 98
Macracantha arcuata
Group: Spiders
Height: 3.5 cm (1 in)
Location: Asia

Brown-lipped snail, page 100
Cepaea nemoralis
Group: Slugs and snails
Length: 3.5 cm (1 in)
Location: Europe

Giant frog-legged beetle, page 102
Sagra longicollis
Group: Beetles
Length: 3.5 cm (1 in)
Location: Southeast Asia

Glorious scarab, page 104
Chrysina gloriosa
Group: Beetles
Length: 3 cm (1 in)
Location: Southern North America

Spotted-wing antlion, page 106
Euroleon nostras
Group: Lacewings and antlions
Length: 3 cm (1 in)
Location: Northern Africa, western Asia,
and Europe

Wasp mantidfly, page 108
Climaciella brunnea
Group: Lacewings and antlions
Length: 3 cm (1 in)
Location: North America

Shocking pink dragon millipede, page 110
Desmoxytes purpurosea
Group: Millipedes
Length: 3 cm (1 in)
Location: Thailand

Giant robber fly, page 114
Microstylum helenae
Group: Flies
Length: 3 cm (1 in)
Location: Southern Africa

Violet oil beetle, page 116
Meloe violaceus
Group: Beetles
Length: 3 cm (1 in)
Location: Northern Africa,
western Asia, and Europe

Bullet ant, page 118
Paraponera clavata
Group: Ants, bees, and wasps
Length: 3 cm (1 in) queen and worker
Location: Central America and South America

Black and yellow mud dauber, page 120
Sceliphron caementarium
Group: Ants, bees, and wasps
Length: 2.8 cm (1 in)
Location: North America

Striped scorpionfly, page 122
Panorpa nuptialis
Group: Scorpionflies
Length: 2.7 cm (1 in)
Location: North America

Giraffe weevil, page 124
Trachelophorus giraffa
Group: Beetles
Length: 2.6 cm (1 in)
Location: Madagascar

Granulated isopod, page 126
Armadillidium granulatum
Group: Woodlice
Length: 2.5 cm (1 in)
Location: Spain

Silverfish, page 128
Lepisma saccharinum
Group: Silverfish
Length: 2.5 cm (1 in)
Location: Worldwide, except the Arctic
and Antarctic

Common glowworm, page 130
Lampyris noctiluca
Group: Beetles
Length: 2.5 cm (1 in)
Location: Asia and Europe

Giant strong-nosed stink bug, page 132
Alcaeorrhynchus grandis
Group: True bugs
Length: 2.5 cm (1 in)
Location: Southern North America and
northern South America

Torreya trapdoor spider, page 134
Cyclocosmia torreya
Group: Spiders
Legspan: 2.5 cm (1 in)
Location: Eastern North America

Blue carpenter bee, page 136
Xylocopa caerulea
Group: Ants, bees, and wasps
Length: 2.3 cm (0.9 in)
Location: Southern Asia and
Southeast Asia

Meadow grasshopper, page 138
Chorthippus parallelus
Group: Grasshoppers
Length: 2.3 cm (0.9 in)
Location: Western Asia
and Europe

**Golden-bloomed grey
longhorn beetle, page 140**
Agapanthia villosoviridescens
Group: Beetles
Length: 2.2 cm (0.9 in)
Location: Western Asia and Europe

Japanese giant water bug, page 142
Appasus japonicus
Group: True bugs
Length: 2.1 cm (0.8 in)
Location: Eastern Asia

Common green lacewing, page 146
Chrysoperla carnea
Group: Lacewings and antlions
Length: 2 cm (0.8 in)
Location: Europe

Namib desert beetle, page 148
Onymacris unguicularis
Group: Beetles
Length: 2 cm (0.8 in)
Location: Southern Africa

European honeybee, page 150
Apis mellifera
Group: Ants, bees, and wasps
Length: 2 cm (0.8 in) queen,
1.5 cm (0.6 in) worker
Location: Worldwide, except the Arctic
and Antarctic

Wheel spider, page 152
Carparachne aureoflava
Group: Spiders
Legspan: 2 cm (0.8 in)
Location: Southern Africa

Gold-necked carrion beetle, page 154
Nicrophorus tomentosus
Group: Beetles
Length: 1.9 cm (0.7 in)
Location: North America

Red velvet ant, page 156
Dasymutilla occidentalis
Group: Ants, bees, and wasps
Length: 1.9 cm (0.7 in)
Location: Southern North America

Australian honeypot ant, page 158
Camponotus inflatus
Group: Ants, bees, and wasps
Length: 1.8 cm (0.7 in) replete
Location: Australia

Bolas spider, page 160
Ordgarius furcatus
Group: Spiders
Legspan: 1.5 cm (0.6 in)
Location: Australia

Common earwig, page 162
Forficula auricularia
Group: Earwigs
Length: 1.5 cm (0.6 in)
Location: Northern Africa, western Asia, Europe, New Zealand, and North America

Pied hoverfly, page 164
Scaeva pyrastri
Group: Flies
Length: 1.5 cm (0.6 in)
Location: Northern Africa, Asia, Europe, and North America

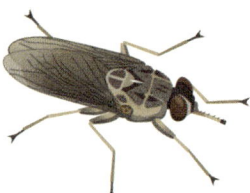

Tsetse fly, page 166
Glossina morsitans
Group: Flies
Length: 1.4 cm (0.6 in)
Location: Central and western Africa

Seven-spot ladybird, page 168
Coccinella septempunctata
Group: Beetles
Length: 1.3 cm (0.5 in)
Location: Northern Africa, Asia, and Europe

Red weaver ant-mimicking spider, page 170
Myrmarachne plataleoides
Group: Spiders
Length: 1.2 cm (0.5 in)
Location: Southern Asia and Southeast Asia

Common horsefly, page 172
Haematopota pluvialis
Group: Flies
Length: 1.2 cm (0.5 in)
Location: Asia and Europe

Two-coloured mason bee, page 174
Osmia bicolor
Group: Ants, bees, and wasps
Length: 1.2 cm (0.5 in)
Location: Northern Africa, Asia, and Europe

Castor bean tick, page 176
Ixodes ricinus
Group: Ticks
Length: 1.1 cm (0.4 in)
Location: Northern Africa, western Asia, and Europe

Spotted regal sawfly, page 178
Nematus septentrionalis
Group: Ants, bees, and wasps
Length: 1 cm (0.4 in)
Location: Europe

Redback spider, page 180
Latrodectus hasselti
Group: Spiders
Legspan: 1 cm (0.4 in)
Location: Australia

Malaysian stalk-eyed fly, page 182
Cyrtodiopsis whitei
Group: Flies
Length: 8 mm (0.3 in)
Location: Southern Asia and Southeast Asia

Acorn weevil, page 184
Curculio glandium
Group: Beetles
Length: 8 mm (0.3 in)
Location: Europe

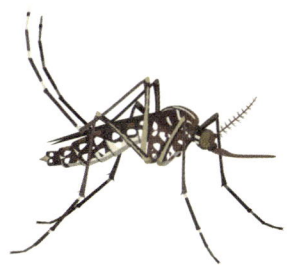

Yellow fever mosquito, page 186
Aedes aegypti
Group: Flies
Length: 7 mm (0.3 in)
Location: Africa

Golden tortoise beetle, page 190
Charidotella sexpunctata
Group: Beetles
Length: 7 mm (0.3 in)
Location: North America and
South America

Meadow froghopper, page 192
Philaenus spumarius
Group: True bugs
Length: 7 mm (0.3 in)
Location: Northern Africa, Asia,
and Europe

Sea skater, page 194
Halobates zephyrus
Group: True bugs
Length: 6 mm (0.2 in)
Location: Eastern Australia

Bristle-tailed planthopper, page 196
Aplos simplex
Group: True bugs
Length: 5 mm (0.2 in)
Location: Eastern North America

Cochineal, page 198
Dactylopius coccus
Group: True bugs
Length: 5 mm (0.2 in)
Location: Southern North America and
northern South America

Slender springtail, page 200
Orchesella flavescens
Group: Springtails
Length: 5 mm (0.2 in)
Location: Europe

Pea aphid, page 202
Acyrthosiphon pisum
Group: True bugs
Length: 4 mm (0.2 in)
Location: Northern Africa, Asia,
and Europe

House pseudoscorpion, page 204
Chelifer cancroides
Group: Pseudoscorpions
Length: 4 mm (0.2 in)
Location: Africa, Australia, Europe,
and North America

Banana lacewing bug, page 206
Stephanitis typica
Group: True bugs
Length: 4 mm (0.2 in)
Location: Southern Asia and
Southeast Asia

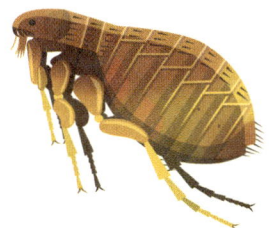

Cat flea, page 208
Ctenocephalides felis
Group: Fleas
Length: 2 mm (0.08 in)
Location: Worldwide, except the Arctic
and Antarctic

Varroa mite, page 210
Varroa destructor
Group: Mites
Length: 2 mm (0.08 in)
Location: Africa, Asia, Europe, and
North America

Penguin Random House

Senior editor **Olivia Stanford**
Project art editor **Charlotte Jennings**
Senior art editors **Ann Cannings, Kanika Kalra, Roohi Rais**
Project editor **Abi Maxwell**
Editorial assistant **Anna Bonnerjea**
Senior picture researcher **Sakshi Saluja**
Pre-production designers **Bimlesh Tiwari, Anita Yadav**
Pre-production image editor **Mohd Rizwan**
Managing art editors **Elle Ward, Ivy Sengupta**
Jacket coordinator **Elin Woosnam**
Production editor **Gillian Reid**
Senior production controller **Ben Radley**
Associate publisher **Gemma Farr**
Delhi creative head **Malavika Talukder**

Consultant **Richard Jones**

First published in Great Britain in 2025 by
Dorling Kindersley Limited
20 Vauxhall Bridge Road,
London SW1V 2SA

The authorised representative in the EEA is
Dorling Kindersley Verlag GmbH. Arnulfstr. 124,
80636 Munich, Germany

MIX
Paper | Supporting
responsible forestry
FSC™ C018179

This book was made with Forest
Stewardship Council™ certified
paper – one small step in DK's
commitment to a sustainable future.
For more information go to
www.dk.com/our-green-pledge

DK would like to thank: Manpreet Kaur for assistance with picture credits;
Gary Ombler for photography; Martin French and The Bug Parc for kindly
allowing us to photograph their animals; Lois Ware for proofreading;
Daniel Long for the feature illustrations; and Angela Rizza for the
pattern and cover illustrations.

About the author: Jess French is a children's author, TV presenter,
and vet. She is also a nature lover who is passionate about bugs.
Her other DK books include: *What a Waste*, *The Book of Brilliant
Bugs*, and *The Animal Body Book*.

Picture credits
The publisher would like to thank the following for their kind permission to reproduce
their photographs: (Key: a-above; b-below/bottom; c-centre; f-far; l-left; r-right; t-top)
4-5 Alamy Stock Photo: Ch'ien Lee / Minden Pictures. **8-9 Shutterstock.com:** Russell Marshall. **10-11 Alamy Stock Photo:** Thomas Marent / Minden Pictures. **18 Todd Burrows. 20 Alamy Stock Photo:** Scenics & Science (tr). **Dreamstime.com:** Palex66 (c). **21 Dreamstime.com:** Viniciussouza06 (crb). **Getty Images / iStock:** Liliboas (tc). **22-23 Dreamstime.com:** Spineback (b). **24-25 Alamy Stock Photo:** blickwinkel / B. Trapp. **28 Julian Kamzol:** (tr, bl). **29 Adobe Stock:** Nynke (br). **32 Alamy Stock Photo:** Andrew Darrington. **34-35 Alamy Stock Photo:** Clarence Holmes Wildlife. **37 Dreamstime.com:** Cathy Keifer. **38 Alamy Stock Photo:** Sabena Jane Blackbird (tl); Neil Phillips (tr); Michael Durham / Minden Pictures (bl); Brais Seara Fernandez / BIA / Minden Pictures (br). **39 Alamy Stock Photo:** Phil Degginger (tl). **Getty Images:** Photodisc / Stefan Mokrzecki (tr). **Shutterstock.com:** Margus Vilbas (tr); yod 67 (b). **40 Alamy Stock Photo:** blickwinkel / G. Kunz. **42-43 Dreamstime.com:** Palex66. **44 Alamy Stock Photo:** Piotr Naskrecki / Minden Pictures (b). **48 Alamy Stock Photo:** Husni Che Ngah / Biosphoto (bl); Nature Picture Library / Alex Hyde (tl); Nature Picture Library / John Abbott (tr). **48-49 Dreamstime.com:** Isselee (bc). **49 Adobe Stock:** Stéphane Bidouze (tl). **Alamy Stock Photo:** Genevieve Vallee (tr); Ian West (cr). **Dreamstime.com:** Mauro Rodrigues (br). **50-51 Alamy Stock Photo:** Thomas Marent / Minden Pictures. **52-53 Alamy Stock Photo:** Nature Picture Library / MYN / Gil Wizen. **55 Nicky Bay. 58-59 Bernard Dupont. 62-63 Alamy Stock Photo:** blickwinkel / F. Hecker. **64 Dreamstime.com:** Vasily Menshov. **66-67 123RF.com:** michellesc. **68-69 Alamy Stock Photo:** Mitsuhiko Imamori / Minden Pictures. **70-71 Alamy Stock Photo:** Flake. **72-73 Alamy Stock Photo:** Nature Picture Library / Konrad Wothe. **74-75 David Weiller / www.davidweiller.com. 78-79 Alamy Stock Photo:** Nature Picture Library / Alex Hyde. **80-81 Dr. Alexey Yakovlev. 82-83 Alamy Stock Photo:** imageBROKER / christian zappel. **84-85 Adobe Stock:** Gerry (b). **86-87 Dave Rentz. 88-89 Alamy Stock Photo:** Natural History Museum, London. **90 Alamy Stock Photo:** Jeff Lepore. **92-93 © Arthur Anker. 94-95 Alamy Stock Photo:** George Grall. **97 Alamy Stock Photo:** Maciej Olszewski. **98 naturepl.com:** Alex Hyde. **100 Alamy Stock Photo:** imageBROKER / Christian Hütter. **103 Alamy Stock Photo:** Panther Media GmbH / Derflassuerp. **104 Alamy Stock Photo:** INSADCO GmbH / McPHOTO / BLWS (bl); Jeff Lepore (cla). **Dreamstime.com:** Cosmin Manci (tr). **Science Photo Library:** Pascal Goetgheluck (br). **105 Dreamstime.com:** Marcouliana (b). **106-107 Shutterstock.com:** Rasmuscool99. **108-109 Alamy Stock Photo:** Nature Picture Library / John Abbott. **110-111 Alamy Stock Photo:** Oliver Thompson-Holmes. **112 Alamy Stock Photo:** George Grall (tl); High Speed Nature (ca); John Richmond (br). **naturepl.com:** Steven David Miller (clb). **112-113 Dreamstime.com:** Matthijs Kuijpers (cl). **113 Alamy Stock Photo:** Stuart Wilson / Biosphoto (tr); Rick & Nora Bowers (b). **114-115 naturepl.com:** Piotr Naskrecki. **116-117 naturepl.com:** Thomas Marent. **118 Science Photo Library:** Nicolas Reusens. **120-121 Alamy Stock Photo:** Rolf Nussbaumer Photography. **122-123 naturepl.com:** John Abbott. **124 Alamy Stock Photo:** Nature Picture Library / Kim Taylor. **125 Alamy Stock Photo:** Nature Picture Library / Alex Hyde. **126 Dreamstime.com:** Suriyapong Koktong (tl). **126-127 Alamy Stock Photo:** Larry Doherty (tc). **129 Science Photo Library:** Javier Torrent, VW Pics. **130-131 Alamy Stock Photo:** David Chapman (t). **132 Alamy Stock Photo:** George Grall. **134-135 naturepl.com:** Joel Sartore / Photo Ark. **136-137 Nicky Bay. 138-139 Shutterstock.com:** Arvind Balaraman (tc). **138 Alamy Stock Photo:** blickwinkel / B. Trapp (bl). **139 Alamy Stock Photo:** Nature Picture Library / Ingo Arndt (br). **Science Photo Library:** MYN / Niall Benvie / Nature Picture Library (tr). **140-141 Shutterstock.com:** Ozgur Kerem Bulur. **142-143 naturepl.com:** Nature Production. **144 123RF.com:** isselee (tl). **Depositphotos Inc:** lifeonwhite (b). **naturepl.com:** Martin Dohrn (tr). **145 Alamy Stock Photo:** blickwinkel (crb); Nature Collection (t); Ray Wilson (c); Heidi & Hans-Juergen Koch / Minden Pictures (bl); Nigel Cattlin (bc). **146-147 Alamy Stock Photo:** High Speed Nature. **148-149 Minden Pictures:** Wendy Dennis. **150 naturepl.com:** Ingo Arndt. **152-153 Dreamstime.com:** Ondrej Prosicky. **154-155 Alamy Stock Photo:** Piotr Naskrecki / Minden Pictures. **156 Alamy Stock Photo:** Stuart Wilson / Biosphoto (b). **Chien C. Lee:** (tc). **Shutterstock.com:** IrinaK (cl). **157 Alamy Stock Photo:** Stuart Wilson / Biosphoto (t). **Eric R. Eaton:** (br). **158-159 Alamy Stock Photo:** Mitsuhiko Imamori / Minden Pictures. **161 Alamy Stock Photo:** Nature Picture Library / Lochman Agency. **163 Alamy Stock Photo:** Scenics & Science. **164 Alamy Stock Photo:** Jef Meul / NIS / Minden Pictures. **168-169 Alamy Stock Photo:** Larry Doherty. **171 Alamy Stock Photo:** Mark Moffett / Minden Pictures. **172-173 Science Photo Library:** Wim Van Egmond. **174 naturepl.com:** Solvin Zankl. **176-177 Alamy Stock Photo:** imageBROKER / Matthias Lenke. **178-179 Alamy Stock Photo:** Nigel Cattlin. **180-181 Depositphotos Inc:** kengriffiths.live.com. **182-183 Alamy Stock Photo:** Mark Moffett / Minden Pictures. **184-185 Alamy Stock Photo:** Frank Hecker. **186-187 Alamy Stock Photo:** Heidi & Hans-Juergen Koch / Minden Pictures. **188 Alamy Stock Photo:** Natural History Museum, London (br); Morley Read (c). **Depositphotos Inc:** Tomatito (tl). **Science Photo Library:** CDC (cl). **189 Alamy Stock Photo:** Thomas Marent / Minden Pictures (br). **Dreamstime.com:** Mularczyk (bl). **Science Photo Library:** (tr); Stuart Wilson (tc). **190-191 Shutterstock.com:** Prasetyo tiyut. **192 Alamy Stock Photo:** Zoonar / HJ Janda. **194-195 Phil Warburton. 196-197 Justis Scott. 198-199 Alamy Stock Photo:** Kris Hoobaer. **200-201 Adobe Stock:** lukjonis. **203 naturepl.com:** Ingo Arndt. **204-205 Adobe Stock:** Stefan Sollfors. **206-207 Nicky Bay. 208-209 Santiago Siutti. 211 Science Photo Library:** Pascal Goetgheluck. **212 Adobe Stock:** bennytrapp (c/Spider); goopholidon (tc); lukjonis (crb/Orchesella). **Alamy Stock Photo:** Ch'ien Lee / Minden Pictures (crb/Worm); Stefan Sollfors (cr); Nature Picture Library / Alex Hyde (cb). **Depositphotos Inc:** EWTC (c); HenrikL (crb/tick). **Dreamstime.com:** Digitalimagined (cr/Silverfish); Viter8 (cra/earwig); Verastuchelova (crb). **Shutterstock.com:** Arvind Balaraman (cra); yod 67 (tr). **213 Alamy Stock Photo:** George Grall (cla); Piotr Naskrecki / Minden Pictures (ca/Beetles); Terry Mathews (c); Oliver Thompson-Holmes (cb); Nature Picture Library / Alex Hyde (bc). **Depositphotos Inc:** imagebrokermicrostock (cra). **Dreamstime.com:** Aetmeister (ca); Ashleylswanson (tc); Mr.smith Chetanachan (tr); Iamtkb (ca/Damselfly). **naturepl.com:** John Abbott (tr/Scorpionfly). **Nicky Bay:** (tl)

Cover images: *Front:* **Alamy Stock Photo:** blickwinkel / B. Trapp cb, blickwinkel / H. Bellmann / F. Hecker cla, DEEPU SG clb, imageBROKER / christian zappel tl, Ch'ien Lee / Minden Pictures cra, Nature Picture Library / Ingo Arndt ca; **Dreamstime.com:** Marcouliana crb, Nymphalyda crb/ (ladybird); **Nicky Bay:** tr